Other versions of this book are available
In French for North America:
La voiture électrique, c'est maintenant ! ISBN   978-2-930940-17-5 (hard-copy)
   dllpresse.ca/a/livres/la-voiture-electrique-cest-maintenant/

In French or English for Europe:
La voiture électrique, c'est maintenant ! ISBN   978-2-930940-15-1 (hard-copy)
The Electric Car, Here and Now!   ISBN   978-2-930940-19-9 (hard-copy)
   nowfuture-editions.com/produit/la-voiture-electrique/

© **Now Future Éditions ASBL**, Liège, Belgium 2019
   info@nowfuture-editions.com

Original title: *La voiture électrique, C'est maintenant !*
Editorial coordination: Patrick Bartholomé and Wendy Nève
English translation: Gabrielle Leyden (www.mount-n-muse.com)
Proofreading: Tim Harrup and Marc Bage
Layout: Colette Michel
Front cover: La boîte de Pandore (laboitedepandore.ca)
Inside illustrations and photograph of the author on the back cover:
©Benjamin Golinvaux (bgolinvaux.artstation.com)
Photographs provided by contributors acknowledged at the end of the volume.
All non-copyrighted photographs are by the author or in the public domain.

ISBN 978-1-0901-2146-2

Printed by Kindle Direct Publishing, USA.

The Electric Car
Here and Now!

Benoît Michel

Translated from the French
by **Gabrielle Leyden**

Original title: **La voiture électrique**, C'est maintenant !

By the same author:

L'animation de bouche des acteurs de synthèse, Digimedia (1994)

CD-ROM "3D Animation", éd. Neurones Production (1994)

Petit Vademecum de l'éditeur électronique, éd. Neurones Production (1994)

"Digital cinema: Revolution or Evolution", in *Film Journal International* (Aug 2001)

Similar Dreams "Multimodal interfaces in our future life" (Chapter 8 only), éd. PUL (2005)

Digital Cinema Perspectives (layout and parts) by the IP-Racine Consortium, éd. B.C.M. (2006)

La Stéréoscopie Numérique, éd. Eyrolles (2011)

Digital Stereoscopy, éd. StereoscopyNews (2013)

Video 3D, Capture, Traitement et Diffusion (Chapter 17), éd. Hermès-Lavoisier (2013)

Consult the exhaustive bibliography at:

benoitmichel.be/perso/pages/bibliographie.html

Table of contents

Introduction

Electric cars have become a fashionable subject of conversation. We talk about them a lot, even though we see very few of them on the road.

Television, Internet, and smartphones are omnipresent in our daily lives, and these innovations were adopted en masse across the planet in the space of a single generation. Each of them upset society as a whole in just a score of years. Over this period, the population's take-up of one of these innovations went from 1 to 99%. In 2019, electric cars account for close to 2% of the cars sold in the world. This raises a serious question, namely: Is the electric car the next iPhone™? And will 99% of us be driving cars that do not burn fossil fuels by the year 2040?

That, in any event, is what several governments, such as those of France and Sweden, have decided to impose on the population. Some large cities, such as London, are already using bans or dissuasive taxes to discourage the use of polluting vehicles in city centers, thereby encouraging users to switch to electric propulsion. Moreover, in the wake of "Dieselgate" and the huge media coverage of this scandal, more and more drivers are themselves wondering about the pollution that their engines generate and looking for alternative solutions.

Is the matter thus in the bag? We can't be sure, for countless innovations wither and die instead of flowering. Why have only a fraction of today's drivers decided to go electric? And why are automakers so discreet about the matter in their advertising? Why is the balance between the pros and cons suddenly tilting the other way? What upheavals will then ensue?

Why do drivers contemplating the purchase of an electric or rechargeable (plug-in) hybrid vehicle often back off at the last moment? More than half of them admit that it's because of a lack of information on the subject and the lack of answers that they get to the questions they put to the dealers, who often know little more than the customers.

Our knowledge of the "electric car" phenomenon is limited for the most part to articles that skim the subject from a great height or focus on one or the other specific detail. Documents that demystify all the facets are very rare. The goal of this book is precisely to fill this gap, to tackle the various aspects of this mobility revolution and raise the veil on the surprises in store for drivers in the years to come.

Electric propulsion – a real innovation   1

The electric car is worming its way more and more into discussions and publications about mobility and global warming. Finding a car magazine that does not raise the subject in each issue is nigh impossible. And yet we see no more than a couple of dozen driving around our towns on any given day. The explanation for this difference is that electric cars are the breakthrough innovation of the moment!

All great innovations follow the same pattern: a more-or-less speedy startup, then a steadily rising rate of adoption until it has been adopted by a majority of the market, and finally a final slow-down as the last resistance finally gives way. Over the years, this entire process has taken less and less time: sixty years for the telephone, forty years for the radio, twenty years for television, fifteen years for the Internet, and ten years for smartphones. The adoption of an innovation such as the telephone or electric car depends on dozens of different factors, but the principles are always the same: The innovation ushers in attractive new possibilities, the advantages increasingly outweigh the drawbacks, the grapevine spreads the information virally, and the market's growth pulls the prices down because of competition and improvements in the product itself.

Of course, not all innovations meet with the success that their creators hope for. Think of 3D television, for example. The sets' manufacturers sang their praises just ten years ago, but their advantages did not suffice to offset the inconvenience of having to wear special glasses for viewing, and the public did not hop on board. Why might the electric car have a better chance of succeeding?

The discovery of the lithium ion battery is what put the electric car back in the limelight. The fact that these batteries are ten times more efficient than lead batteries finally makes

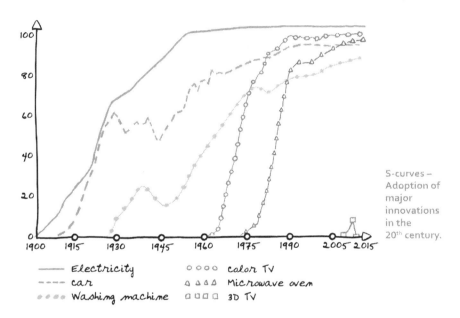

S-curves –
Adoption of major innovations in the 20th century.

──────── Electricity   ○ ○ ○ ○ Color TV
── ── ── car   △ △ △ △ Microwave oven
● ● ● ● Washing machine □ □ □ □ 3D TV

them serious rivals of gasoline and diesel fuel. Once this efficiency hurdle has been cleared, the other features of electric propulsion – less noise and pollution, mechanical simplicity, cheaper cost of use, and driving ease – become so many advantages. These are already impressive advantages in their own right, but when placed in today's context of combating pollution and climate change, they tie in almost perfectly with society's need to reduce its fossil fuel consumption and the rising curve of local renewable power generation through wind turbines and photovoltaic (PV) panels.

Breakthrough innovation

By definition, a breakthrough innovation offers better performance than the solution already in place for a given application and often ushers in new options that are impossible to provide with existing technology. The tipping point – the decisive moment as of which users no longer want the old technology – occurs when the cost of the new technology becomes competitive with that of the existing technology.

According to many experts, the tipping point for electric cars should be reached around 2022-25 at the very latest. The factors that will bring the prices of electric cars down to the range of Internal Combustion Engine (ICE) cars of the same category are cheaper batteries, financial incentives for buyers, increased production volumes, and, of course, new antipollution regulations.

The environmental standards foreseen in the next few years in the wake of the Dieselgate scandal will inevitably increase the complexity and thus the price of ICE cars while excise duties and other taxes on fossil fuels will continue to rise. This will help to tip the scales in favor of electric propulsion all the more quickly.

The S-curve

The innovators who make up the first 2% of a new product's users are attracted by novelties, even if their prices are high. They are followed by the "early adopters," who are convinced by the positive examples that they see and looming price reductions. Finally, the success of an innovation is confirmed – this is the "point of no return" – when the explorers

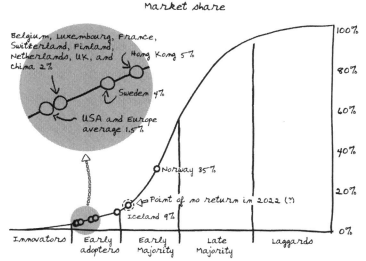

The S-curve of new electric vehicle sales.

The tipping point

The point of no return will occur when the purchase prices of electric cars fall to the same levels as those of their ICE counterparts. This moment is fast approaching, but what do the experts say? According to Martin Eberhard, Tesla co-founder and consultant for Volkswagen USA, this point will be reached in 2022. For the investment bank J.P. Morgan Cazenove, 2022 is a credible date and sales should snowball thereafter. J.P. Morgan Cazenove's analysts believe that the fear of losing resale value on their old cars will cause many consumers to rush to buy electric cars even before the tipping point is achieved. They thus predict that electric cars will account for 35% of the market in 2025 and 48% in 2030.

Government policies can speed things up by offering tax incentives and promoting the necessary infrastructure. So it is that Norway was the farthest along the curve in late 2018 with a 35% take-up rate, a figure that climbs to 50% if plug-in hybrids are included.

are joined by the public at large, which can finally see the technological advantages that can be enjoyed at competitive prices. If we imagine the S-curve of the electric car market's growth between 2015 and 2040, this threshold will be reached around 2022-25.

Mitigating the greenhouse effects of CO_2 emissions into the air calls for reducing the use of natural gas, gasoline, and diesel fuel drastically. The governments of practically all the world's countries have embarked on this path, with the (maybe temporary) exception of the United States. France and Canada promised to stop selling ICE (Internal Combustion Engine) passengers cars as early as 2040. Denmark and Israël are even more in a hurry with a 2030 deadline! The governments of Sweden, India, and China have similar plans and are offering sometimes substantial EV purchase bonuses. More and more large cities, such as London, are banning polluting vehicles or taxing them heavily. So, in China, the buyer of a light electric vehicle can get up to US$10,350[1] (CAN$13,500) in subsidies.

With its aggressive pollution-control policy, China leads the pack of electric car-using countries and hopes to have more than 7 million new energy vehicles (NEVs) on its roads by 2025.

---

1. *The euro-to-dollar conversion rates used in this edition are appoximately the ones that were in effect on Feb. 1st 2019, i.e., €1.00 = US$1.15 and CAN$1.50.*

There are more than 500,000 NEVs on the road in the U.S., but Norway is at the head of the class in terms of the percentage of electric vehicle sales. In March 2014, Norway was the first country in the world to have electric cars reach 1% of cars on the road and by December 2018 electric cars already accounted for 52% of the new car market. It must be said that in Norway electric cars are exempt from the road tax; they have their own lanes on urban highways and free parking; they are exempt from paying tolls; they benefit from State purchase subsidies, including exoneration of the 25% tax until 2020; and the sale of ICE cars will be banned starting in 2025. The Norwegians now even have an infrastructure problem: It's becoming hard to find charging stations that are not fully occupied!

The International Energy Agency (IEA) is encouraging its twenty-nine member countries to cap the global temperature rise at 2°C. To achieve this, it has called for electrifying means of transportation and increasing the share of renewables in power generation. To meet this 2° target, new electric car sales must rise 35% each year until at least 2025, meaning that governments must step up their policies to support electrification. Ireland just joined the club of countries that will soon ban the sale of fossil fuel-powered vehicles: This 2018 decision will go into effect in 2030. What is more, Ireland intends to ban all ICE vehicles from the roads as of 2045.

The Volkswagen I.D. prototype, scheduled for rollout in 2020.

More than thirty countries and regions, including France, Belgium, India, Quebec, and the United States, have followed China's example and currently give the buyers of electric or hybrid vehicles purchase bonuses or tax rebates and subsidize the establishment of public charging stations.

More and more automakers are banking on a boom in electric propulsion. Tesla, the best-known maker of 100% electric vehicles in the world, took in more than 400,000 US$1,000 down payments on its Model 3 before even releasing the car on the market in the second half of 2017 and has announced that it wants to put a million Teslas on the roads between now and 2020 at the very latest.

©Volkswagen

A shot of Volkswagen's future I.D. range.

The major traditional automakers have also announced their targets: Porsche asserts that 50% of its output will be electric or hybrid in 2030, Volkswagen has announced one million electric cars in its future I.D. range in 2025, and Volvo has declared that it is ending its R&D on ICE vehicles and will be selling only electric or hybrid vehicles starting in 2019.

However, the major automakers' current public statements often contradict their short- and medium-term intentions

The two faces of carmakers

Our major traditional automakers are currently devoting a mere 2% of their marketing budgets to purely electric propulsion. This fact alone shows more of a concern to restore reputations tarnished by the Dieselgate scandals than a true desire to change.

The VDA (German Association of the Automotive Industry) represents automakers controlling 20% of global car production. Its president, Matthias Wissmann, announced in July 2017 that its members would be spending 40 billion euros on research into alternative propulsion over the next two years, adding that 100 electric car models would be on the market in Germany by 2020. However, in the same announcement he stressed that electricity was but one of the options being investigated, alongside natural gas and biofuel. "Despite the controversy surrounding diesel fuel, the latter remains necessary to meet the foreseen CO_2 emissions quotas. And it is also very clear that gasoline and diesel fuel remain the keys to mobility in the years to come, with a potential 10- to 15-percent decrease in their consumption."

and plans. Indeed, let's not forget that they have invested dozens of billions of dollars in technologies and plants dedicated to churning out internal combustion engines and abandoning all this before it has paid for itself simply is not possible. These declarations may be intended (at least partially) more to modernize their images than to embody a true change of course.

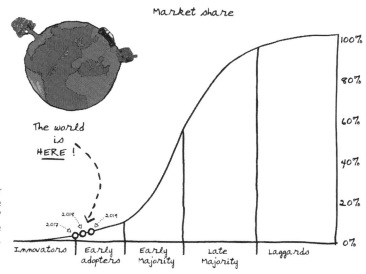

Market share

The world is HERE!

The electric car is entering the "early adopters" phase of the S-curve.

Innovators | Early adopters | Early Majority | Late Majority | Laggards

2017 · 2018 · 2019

100% 80% 60% 40% 20% 0%

The S-curve that the take-up of electric cars in the world is following is still in its very first phase. It is drawing near the first bend where an acceleration is starting to be felt. This is also the time when the public at large wonders and asks questions to learn more from the early adopters who have already taken the plunge.

Conversations revolve more and more often around variations on the same theme, namely, "Yes, it sounds great, but it will always be too expensive" or "It's good for some people, but not for me." All of this is reminiscent of the early days of the cell phone: "Yes, indeed, it might be useful at times, but an iPhone costs so much more than my good old landline," "In any event, the screen is too small to look at pictures and sending them over the Internet would take hours," and so on. Electric car owners, for their part, tout above all how pleasant and easy their cars are to drive and their silence, never mind the absence of gas or diesel fumes and odors. These advantages are hard for people who have never tried electric vehicles to grasp but, at the end of the day, such "finer points" are often much more important for them than the operating cost per mile or performance stats.

What shape will this S-curve finally take?

It is still very hard to say with certainty at what date the S-curve will approach the 100% mark, given that so far only the start of the bottom curve (2010-18) is known. Various analysts have released estimates, with those of oil companies being the lowest and those of the more active market players, such as Tesla and Bloomberg New Energy Finance, being among the highest.

With over 5,000,000 electric vehicles on the road in spring 2019, and one-third of them over only the past twelve months, the first percent of the global automobile market has been exceeded. Plotting the rest of the curve is difficult, for a number of reasons.

Negative factors: Prices that are too high, an insufficiently diversified supply, no electric pick-ups or SUVs, a scanty public charging station infrastructure, and so on. And what overnight charging solution exists for drivers who do not have their own garages?

Positive factors: Prices are coming down, ranges are increasing, the supply is getting broader from one year to the next, public and company charging stations are spreading, etc.

Still, dozens of events are likely to upset these developments. History is full of surprises and there is no reason why the car market should escape this rule.

Among the potential barriers to the growth in the number of electric cars are above all possible technology-related problems, such as a crisis in the availability of the exotic materials used. The lithium used in the batteries is present everywhere, but lithium batteries also contain some rarer elements, such as nickel and cobalt, albeit in small amounts. These metals are

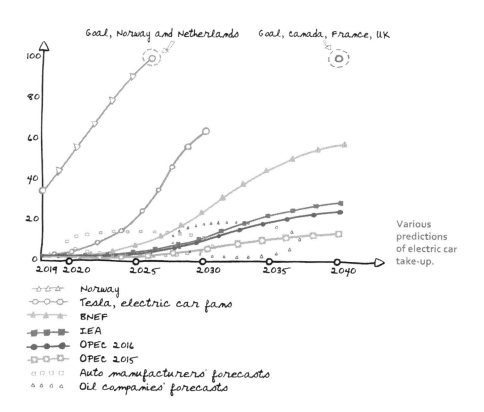

Various predictions of electric car take-up.

Cars in figures

There are about 1 billion passenger cars on Earth, or approximately one car for 7.6 people. Around one in every 230 cars is an electric or plug-in hybrid vehicle. There are currently 4.3 million such vehicles on the road, or 0.43 % of the global car fleet.

Private cars	1,000,000,000	100.00%
Electric cars	4,300,000	0.43%

Some 80 million new cars are sold each year. The average lifespan of a passenger car is 12.5 years.

The electric vehicle global market share (including plug-in hybrids) is rising strongly: it was 1.5% in 2017 and 2.3% in 2018. Forecasts for 2019 are total sales of more than 3 million units, or 3.8% of total new car sales.

not as rare as gold and platinum, but are nevertheless at the mercy of geopolitical crises and financial market speculation.

We can also mention the legitimate reluctance of drivers mindful of the ethical issues surrounding the provision of battery components, especially the case of cobalt. More than half of the world's cobalt reserves are located in the Democratic Republic of Congo (DRC), and 20% of DRC's cobalt comes from cottage-industry mines that Amnesty International criticizes for deplorable working conditions, child labor, and little respect for the environment. Luckily, initiatives such as the Responsible Cobalt Initiative (RCI) are lashing out against such practices. The supplier of Samsung's SDI lithium ion batteries is one of the RCI's founders.

American and European laws are favorable to electrification in varying degrees, but the subsidies and tax rebates that support electric vehicles today will not last forever. They are there only to support the startup phase. What is more, as time goes by and the number of ICE cars on the road decreases and the excise taxes on fuel and pollution taxes that governments collect shrink commensurately, the government penchant for taxation is very likely to wake up and spread to the new vehicles as well.

Another possible risk is permanently cheap oil or a surge in the already powerful oil lobby, whose disinformation campaigns about global warming and the use of fossil fuels could have considerable impact, especially in oil-producing countries.

What about the factors that could boost the growth of the electric car market? The main one is an electric versus ICE car price comparison. Electric car prices are falling and will continue to decrease. Currently, half of this price is due to the cost of the batteries, and intense research efforts in this area explain the steady decrease in battery prices. On the other hand, internal combustion engines and their hybrid variations are becoming more and more complex and expensive to manufacture, if only to meet increasingly stringent environmental standards.

City policies are another factor in favor of replacing the ICE with electricity. Many cities around the world belong to the C40 platform (www.c40.org). This is a global movement of more than 100 major cities, such as Boston, Los Angeles, New York, Montreal, and London, that are adamant about combating pollution and global warming by adopting low-emissions strategies and regulations encouraging the use of clean vehicles.

Since October 2017 all vehicles driving in central London's Congestion Charge Zone must comply with severe

The first fully-electric double-decker bus put in service in London in 2016.

pollution standards or pay a daily congestion charge of £10 (roughly US$13, CAN$17). Driving a diesel around in central London every day thus costs about US$5,000 a year! And the mayor of London, Sadiq Khan, has proposed extending this zone gradually and turning it into an Ultra Low Emission Zone (ULEZ) starting in April 2019. The surcharge for ICE vehicles will then rise to £12.50 a day, or US$6,000 a year. This policy is making the big fleet operators, such as Transport for London, stop and think. Transport for London, which runs London's well-known red double-deckers, is already starting to electrify its fleet. Mr. Khan wants 100% of the taxis and mass transit in London to be electric by 2037 and to ban all ICE engines from central London starting in 2040.

Not only are the drivers of electric vehicles who regularly drive into central London exempt from the congestion charge, but they also get reduced-rate parking: *Pay for ten minutes, stay the day*. What is more, they have access to 1,500 charging points for up to four hours free of charge. Another strategy is being considered in Stuttgart, Germany, that of banning diesel engines from the city center as soon as pollution exceeds a pre-established threshold. Just the fact that this ban is likely to make downtown Stuttgart inaccessible to them many days a year is making commuters and delivery fleets think about clean solutions, such as hybrid and electric cars.

The importance of China

China's policy weighs heavily on the automobile market's scales. While China was selling 1 million cars in 2010, it is now churning out 25 million light cars in one year (2017). Having failed to carve out a market share with an outdated ICE technology and faced with intolerable pollution levels, China is taking every measure at its disposal to become the world leader in the New Energy Vehicle (NEV) sector. Its centralized, interventionist policies give it means on a par with its ambitions, and it is now urging foreign automakers to set up plants in free zones where they can take advantage

Traffic is the leading cause of urban pollution in China.

of cheap local subcontractors without being forced to share their secrets with local manufacturers.

The Chinese government's command-and-control policy has set a tight calendar aimed at manufacturing 70% of the electric vehicles used in China domestically as of 2020, with these vehicles accounting for 10% of total sales. However, unlike Western automakers, the Chinese are exhibiting an impressive will to conquer this new market.

The three main suppliers of electric vehicles in China are Beijing Automotive (BAIC), BYD, and Geely. The last-named is better known to us for having bought Lotus, London Taxi International, Volvo, and Lynk. Geely's CEO, Li Shufu, is the largest private shareholder in the Daimler-Mercedes-Benz group (the Chinese businessman laid €9 billion on the table in 2018), which may explain Mercedes's recent interest in selling electric cars in China.

BYD's General Manager, Wang Chuanfu, declared in September 2017 his intention to produce only electric vehicles in twelve years' time. It must be pointed out that BYD is the number one manufacturer of lithium batteries and signed an agreement with Daimler to co-manufacture electric cars locally. Finally, not wishing to be left out in the

Fossil fuels and pollution go hand in hand.

cold, the head of the BAIC group, Xu Heyi, has announced his group's intention to be the most active supplier of electric cars sold on the Chinese market in 2019 and help achieve the target of 7 million sales in 2025. Tesla has started to build a factory in Shanghai that is expected to produce 500,000 electric cars and SUVs per year for the Chinese market.

With more than 550,000 light electric vehicles rolling off the assembly lines in 2017 and close to 1 million in 2018, the Chinese market's annual growth rate of 40% seems to be a reality. The target of 3,000,000 units sold in 2020 should be achieved or even very likely surpassed.

Meanwhile...

A detail that leaves a stain on the European States' "green" policies is the continued granting of large subsidies to the oil, coal, and gas industries: According to the IMF, government subsidies to the fossil energy sector exceed US$530 billion worldwide each year, and the U.S. contributes more than 11% of this sum, distributing €60 billion to this sector each year! This amount includes 25 billion for transport.

In Europe, a large part of these subsidies was originally intended to promote diesel engines, which supposedly generate less CO_2 than gasoline engines. A fifth of these subsidies goes to help the transition to low-carbon-emissions energy and ends up being distributed to the extractors of fossil energy sources, such as German coal mines and British oil rigs in the North Sea. The European Union and its Member States have promised to end this hypocrisy, which is contrary to the Paris Agreement that they signed, by 2020, but they visibly fear hurting a major sector of the economy.

Simply shifting the huge sums of money paid to the fossil fuel industry to the renewable energy sector could have a clear impact on the diesel engine's attractiveness and adoption of electric propulsion.

The factors that accelerate the S-curve include social pressure. The epitome of the "cool car" in the 1960s-1980s was the sporty convertible. Today, the SUV – a bulky gas-guzzler with a high-riding chassis – is top of the list. However, given the repercussions of Dieselgate, will the powerful, silent, comfortable electric car soon be the most awesome means of transportation in the 21st century?

Why not a straight line?

Innovations follow non-linear trends at both the start and the end of their adoption. That is all because of self-reinforcing influences, *i.e.*, the virtuous circles that tend to accelerate the emergence of new technology and the vicious circles that reinforce old technology's tendency to leave the scene.

The steady drop in battery prices and increases in the electric car's cost-effectiveness are boosting electric car sales volumes. The ensuing economies of scale will push the sales and cost prices down while diversifying the supply. That in turn will increase the sales volume, and so on and so forth. Many such virtuous circles apply to the cars' performances, tax incentives, and charging infrastructure. All of these effects contribute to the first bend in the S-curve.

Inversely, the more electric cars ply our roads, the more difficult it will become to sell used diesel cars, and even gas-burning hybrids will quickly lose value. Their owners will thus get rid of them at low prices faster and faster to cut their losses. That will in turn contribute to the market's collapse and thus reinforce the drop in the ICE's value and strengthen electric car adoption. This trend has already become visible over the past year for second-hand diesel cars that do not meet European Standards 5 and 6. The end of the curve shows a slowing-down of this trend due mainly to the continued use of sturdy, durable cars with low mileage that do not have to be replaced and for which a high cost price per mile is of little importance.

The dynamics of vicious and virtuous circles.

On the other hand, other vicious circles will take root: The fall in ICE production volumes will increase their manufacturing costs and thus their prices. The drop in fuel consumption will lead to higher fuel taxes and excise duties, which will help to depress consumption even further, and so on. Social pressure against dirty vehicles will follow the same pattern: Being one of the last people on your block to drive a car that "smokes" will create bad blood with your neighbors and you'll tend to get rid of your "dirty clunker" earlier than you planned. Since fewer and fewer dirty cars will be seen in the streets, the pressure on the last diehards will increase accordingly.

The virtuous and vicious circles' effects combine to precipitate events and turn the simple straight line of shortsighted forecasters into an exponential curve that will reach its apogee much sooner.

A tale of horse manure

In studying the S-curve of electric car adoption we cannot help but make the parallel with the automobile's adoption at the start of the 20th century. Cars were much rarer in 1900 than electric vehicles are today, cost a pretty penny, and broke down all the time. What is more, New York City alone had to clean its streets of more than 1,000 metric tons of horse manure a day!

©Metroline

5th Avenue, NY, in 1900. If you look closely, you'll spot a horseless carriage along the left sidewalk!

The same 5th Avenue in 1925. Not a horse in sight!

When the Model T, which would revolutionize the world, rolled off the assembly lines in 1908, its launch price was a fairly affordable US$850 dollars (or US$21,600, CAN$28,000 in 2019 currency). However, the invention of the assembly line in itself was an important-enough innovation to trigger various virtuous circles that reduced the car's cost price below the price of a horse, which remained just as expensive as before, soiled the stables and streets just as much, and was limited by a range of some twenty miles a day.

Thirteen years later, in 1921, Ford was selling a million Model T's a year and New Yorkers were delighted by the disappearance of horse manure from the streets. By 1925 middle-class Americans were no longer waiting for their last horses to die in order to replace them with cars and Ford was selling almost 2 million Model T's a year at less than 300 dollars a piece.

Neither the lack of service stations and asphalted streets nor its high price prevented the car from taking over in a mere fifteen or so years. A century later, the shift to electric vehicles seems much easier, as the car has become much simpler and more robust and setting up the necessary charging infrastructure will be much less expensive than building oil refineries was in the early 20th century.

You cannot foresee everything...

Breakthrough innovations other than the replacement of the ICE by electric motors could also come along and completely reshuffle the cards. So, the shared driverless car is an increasingly likely "innovation on the innovation" of the electric car. The mass roll-out of self-driving robot cars will be possible only in conjunction with electric vehicles, which are the only ones that can provide the necessary reactivity features. Technology forecaster Tony Seba of Stanford University has even imagined that the advent of self-driving cars will follow on the heels of widely available electric cars. This should not only accelerate their adoption, but also greatly reduce the demand for individual passenger cars and thus increase the proportion of electric cars in the global fleet.

Not only is the year when the S-curve reaches 100% unknown, but it is also of little importance. However, the next decade will more than likely see the curve becoming more and more precise as the elements that we have just mentioned interact. And many clues point to the clear possibility that the revolution will take place much faster than is generally thought today.

And afterwards?

Once diesel and gas engines disappear from the new car market, what will happen to all the old cars that are still in service?

Let's not forget the gigantic size of the global automotive industry: More than 1 billion light vehicles are on the road around the world and the number is likely to rise even more over the next ten years! Today's cars have far-from-negligible lifespans and the relatively low replacement rate of the global fleet of cars will have an obvious consequence: Even when we reach the point where only electric vehicles are sold, the share of ICE cars in circulation will not fall to zero overnight. It will probably take another score or so of years for them to reach the ends of their lives and/or all be recycled, which will bring us to around 2050 or 2060. However, it is just as possible that the ICE cars that are not sent to museums may become unsellable scrap in less than fifteen years, for the possibilities of selling an ICE car at a decent price on the used-car market will melt away well before we reach the end of the S-curve.

The global context

Global warming is an increasingly obvious reality. The Paris Agreement on Climate that was signed in 2016 united all the countries in the world around the vital need to reduce greenhouse gas emissions. "But," you may ask, "how should we see Donald Trump's decision to withdraw the United States from the Paris Agreement?" The protectionist reasons behind the U.S.'s withdrawal from the agreement are known, but their negative effects on the crusade against global warming remain limited, for they are offset by a wide range of support, such as that of Sciencebasedtargets, a private group that includes more than 300 companies (Adobe, Coca-Cola, Dell, Kellogg, and Wal-Mart for starters). Not to be outdone, a slew of U.S. cities and no fewer than fifteen states, led by New York and California, have confirmed their status as parties to the Paris Agreement.

Future disasters linked to global warming can be prevented only if the use of fossil fuels such as oil and coal is cut drastically. The non-CO_2-emitting energy sources that can be used today are either nuclear fission or renewables. The risks and other disadvantages of nuclear energy do not plead in its favor. Consequently, we are basically left with renewables to meet our insatiable energy needs.

The energy that we manage to recover from waterfalls, the wind, and the sun accounts for only a tiny fraction of the energy with which the sun has been flooding the planet for millions of years. Just one percent of this constantly renewed energy could cover all of humankind's energy needs indefinitely. What do all these solutions have in common? They produce usable energy in the form of electricity. We can thus expect huge changes in the distribution of energy around the world in the coming decades: better and smarter electricity grids with a large number of highly scattered sources, local storage facilities, and very different rules and rates from those of today.

Even in less sunny northern states, the increasingly visible presence of wind turbines and solar panels on our roofs is proof that society is aware of the problem and starting to take action.

©Koliri

A wind farm that generates 50 MW on the hills of Patras in Greece.

The renewable energy boom is under way! The cost of installing renewable sources of electricity has fallen over the second decade of the 21st century to levels below those of fossil fuel-fired and nuclear power plants. The "*Big Green Bang*" described by the Financial Times will have – and has already had – major consequences for all sectors of the economy. Fossil fuels are still our main energy source (86% of the

The sun's energy

The sun gives off as much energy each second as 10 billion atomic bombs. The portion that reaches Earth is but a fraction of the whole, but nevertheless amounts to 400 terawatts or about 1,000 times all the electricity generated by all the nuclear power plants on Earth. This energy turns into heat when it comes in contact with the Earth's atmosphere and ground. It drives all the climatic phenomena around the planet, such as rainfall and hurricanes, and we recover a tiny portion of it with the help of hydroelectric turbines, wind turbines, and photovoltaic panels.

total), but things are changing at an incredible pace. In just twenty-five years (1990-2015), during which the consumption of fossil energy sources rose by 70%, that of solar and wind energy rose by more than 1,200%!

The major oil companies are aware of the revolution that has begun and are trying to slow the trend down. However, since the cost prices and costs of building wind turbines and photovoltaic panels have become competitive, it is becoming harder and harder to make a case for oil.

Renewable energy will account for more than 15% of the U.S. energy market in 2019 and is growing faster each year. Twice as much money is being invested in wind power and

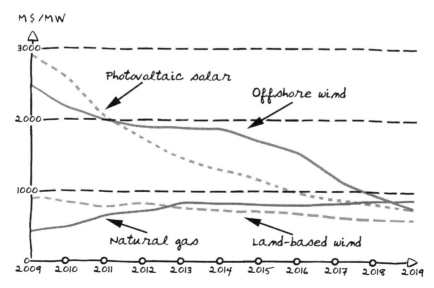

The costs of renewable electricity-generating facilities have fallen steadily and are now below those of natural gas.

PV research as in the fuel sector. Furthermore the combination of batteries with renewable but intermittent wind and sunlight energy will spark even more interest in these increasingly profitable sources.

The worst polluter in the world, China, is one of the first countries to have understood the advantages of the renewable energy revolution. And although CO_2 and global warming are not the Chinese people's chief concern, the rising pol-

The carbon bubble

The term "carbon bubble" is modeled after the "real estate bubble," *i.e.*, the financial crisis that swept over the U.S. from 2007 to 2010. The world's usable fossil fuel resources are limited. The general consensus is that to limit global warming to 2°C, no more than 20% of these total resources must be consumed. At the rate we are going, this will be achieved in twenty years. In other words, all our oil, coal, and gas industries must stop operating in 2040, which means that their value will be nil! The bubble will not burst in 2040, but most likely well before then, as soon as the financial markets discover it is time to divest before oil shares lose all their value. Indeed, why buy shares in an oil company that is spending billions of dollars to prospect for new usable oil fields when its market is declining?

The vicious circle that will take root under these conditions is akin to a bubble bursting because its effects will be felt in the very short range, sometimes over just a few years. When (and not "if") that happens, we shall experience a global economic upheaval. The automakers that do not chose their sides early enough will find themselves bereft of a market and financing. The most foresighted among them that bet on electric motors in time will survive the storm and harvest the fruits that fall off the other side's trees.

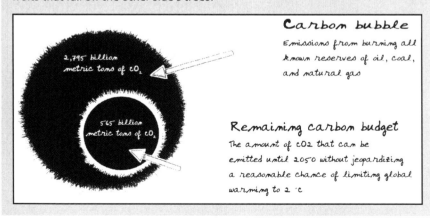

Carbon bubble
Emissions from burning all known reserves of oil, coal, and natural gas

2,795 billion metric tons of CO_2

565 billion metric tons of CO_2

Remaining carbon budget
The amount of CO_2 that can be emitted until 2050 without jeopardizing a reasonable chance of limiting global warming to 2 °c

lution in their major cities has reached critical levels. The intolerable clouds of pollution for which Chinese cities are known should be no more than a bad memory in ten or twenty years' time, for renewable electricity is growing there by leaps and bounds. One-third of the world's existing wind turbines are in China, which is also where you find 25% of the world's PV panels, six of the world's ten leading PV panel manufacturers, and more electric vehicles than in the rest of the world.

The spread of wind power will be limited by the number of suitable sites in each country, with the coastal areas having an advantage because of the possibility of increasing the number of offshore wind turbines near the coastline. The efficiency of PV panels depends heavily on the incident sunlight locally, but the room for improvement is still huge.

According to estimates, renewables will account for more than 50% of energy consumption on Earth by 2030, but China will achieve this threshold before Europe: It had already achieved the ambitious targets that it had set for itself for 2020 by 2017.

And transportation in all that?

The transportation sector is a very important part of the economy. It accounts for about a quarter of global energy consumption. The only way to make land transportation independent of fossil fuel is to opt for electricity, and thus onboard storage batteries. In many countries, railroads converted to electricity decades ago because they did not have to grapple with the problem of batteries, and they are formidably efficient running this way. However, for vehicles that are not locked into their own sites, such as private cars, buses, and trucks, the picture is completely different, for they have to carry on board all the energy needed for a trip.

Modern cars can cover up to 600 miles (1,000 km) on a small tank of gasoline without being penalized by the vehicle's excessive weight or bulkiness, and their tanks take mere minutes to fill. In contrast, this problem becomes much more

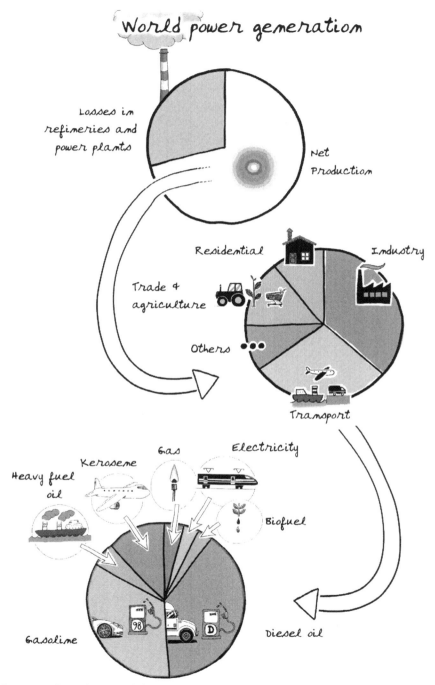

World power generation

Losses in refineries and power plants

Net Production

Residential

Industry

Trade & agriculture

Others

Transport

Gas

Electricity

Kerosene

Heavy fuel oil

Biofuel

Gasoline

Diesel oil

Transportation's place in global energy consumption.

critical with electricity, which is very easy to use but notoriously difficult to store. Luckily for us, batteries have made enormous progress since the invention of the automobile and are continuing to make gains today.

Most of the first cars in history were electric. Gasoline-powered engines had just been invented and were known above all for breaking down and spewing clouds of black smoke! The first "automobile driver's manuals" recommended taking along a tool kit and a few spare parts, such as connecting rods and pistons. The electric motor's robustness, simple build, silence, and lack of noisome emissions contributed to the development of the first cars as of the late 19th century. The main problem for these precursors was their limited range, for the lead batteries that they used were very heavy and discharged quickly! Still, those drawbacks did not prevent the Belgian Camille Jenatzy from being the first racing driver to reach 100 km/h (60 mph) in his electric "torpedo" *Jamais Contente* (Never Satisfied). The year was 1899.

The ads of the time touted not only the electric horseless carriage's simplicity and ease of use, but also its lack of odors: no smelly horse manure or nauseating gasoline fumes!

With the advances made in the gasoline engine, electric cars disappeared from the streets around 1910. They finally

The *Jamais Contente* of 1899. You can glimpse the two motors between the rear wheels. Thanks to the 50 kW that they generated, the car was clocked at 65 mph or 105 km/h.

One of Thomas Parker's
electric horseless carriages
in 1895.

returned to center stage in 1990, under the impetus of CARB (the California Air Resources Board), which required automakers to offer "zero carbon" models on pain of being banned throughout the state. However, it took the oil price crisis of 2000 and above all the advent of the lithium-ion battery, which can store five to ten times more energy than its lead predecessor, to breathe new life into the market.

Tesla's first roadsters were rolled out in 2008. Models produced by many other car makers, such as Nissan, Chevrolet, and Mitsubishi, followed quickly on Tesla's heels.

Given the great gains achieved with lithium batteries, the electric car finally started to make its mark. This was in parallel with scientists and public authorities' awareness of the urgent need to replace fossil fuels with less environmentally harmful solutions.

The public at large, for its part, wants solutions to its problems, not technology for technology's sake. In our increasingly overcrowded cities, people want mobility solutions that meet their needs. That means simplicity, connectivity, and immediate availability. So, it is no coincidence that car-sharing and electric bicycles and motorbikes are joining forces to make life easier in today's major cities. The electric car, which is silent, does not pollute, and could even drive itself one day, fits perfectly into the scheme of things.

The early 21st century will be known in the history books as the period of the advent of the social networks that spread in parallel with mobile phones. Facebook, Twitter, and the other networks are helping greatly to spread ideas and trends. Climate change and the fight against burning fossil fuels are being given more and more space in the social media, where the ground is more than fertile, especially among the members of the "Z" generation that was born with Internet and Facebook. The general feeling that we must save the planet and behave in an environmentally responsible manner is widespread. The electrification of the passenger car fits in this context quite naturally, most often in conjunction with the development of renewables as one way to mitigate global warming.

The current context, which is in favor of reducing greenhouse gas emissions, is combined with the steady concentration of populations in cities and ever-increasing demand for non-polluting mobility. It offers the electric car a great likelihood of becoming the iPhone™ of the 2020s, *i.e.*, the unrivaled new product that will revolutionize and dominate its sector.

More than a fad

The electric car is much more than an ecological fad for rich people. Rather, it is an effective answer to an increasingly urgent need. It has many enormous advantages for society: lower GHG emissions, complete elimination of pollution by fine particles and nitrogen oxides, noise reduction, increased safety, and national budget savings thanks to reductions in oil imports. Its drawbacks – limited range and public charging infrastructure that is still in its infancy – are being reduced each year thanks to research advances and public and private investment.

The inconvenience and pollution to which increased electricity use will lead will be much easier to control than those produced by the millions of ICE cars scattered around the areas where we live. Cleaning up an electric power plant is much easier than getting rid of millions of catalytic converters! And let's not forget that the increasing replacement of fossil fuel-burning power plants by renewable energy sources is combining with electric means of transportation to help us limit the effects of global warming.

The *status quo* with gasoline- or diesel-powered vehicles is simply no longer a credible option. ICE vehicles and the con-

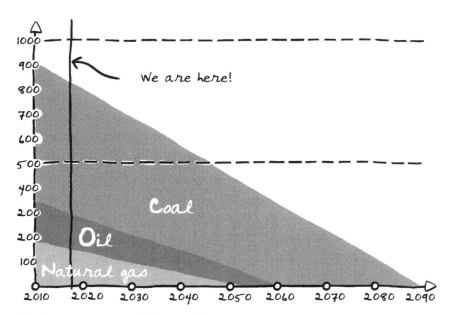

Global energy reserves are falling. Even if new deposits are discovered, they will not be eternal. Reducing our fossil fuel consumption is our only option.

sumption of fossil fuels are inseparable from air, water, and soil pollution and the ensuing negative public health impacts. And let's not forget that fossil fuels are non-renewable resources that will inevitably run out one day. Worldwide, we use 11 billion metric tons of oil a year. At this rate, oil will have disappeared completely by 2052. Or, to be more accurate, in thirty years, the market will not be willing to pay the price that extracting oil will cost. At that point, some ten years of natural gas deposits will remain and a few dozen years of coal deposits. But will people dare to pump or dig up those last reserves, given the pollution that such activity would generate?

Europe does not have enormous energy resources of its own. Europeans will thus be among the first to feel the pinch. For example, the United Kingdom's reasonably accessible crude oil reserves will run out in 2027.

However, the U.S. sits on a vast and almost completely untapped reserve of shale oil, but extracting and refining this resource are costly operations. Consequently, the economic feasibility of tapping this reserve is not guaranteed. What is certain, however, is the enormous amount of ecological damage such exploitation will generate.

What do the financial experts think?

The financial analysts whose opinions cause stock market prices to rise and fall are not the best guides in a context of innovation. Their job is to analyze the current situation and forecast the short-term value trends of the companies listed on the market, not to imagine society's future ten or twenty years down the road. They thus tend to extrapolate (1% growth this year, so then another 1% next year, and yet another 1%, etc.) and revise their forecasts each year to fit current developments. Luckily, some of them study innovative non-linear trends and incorporate them in their forecasts. More and more of the latter back up the figures given above.

The Swiss bank UBS published a report in mid-2017 that predicted the cost price of gasoline-powered cars and electric cars being equal as of 2018, with the trend first taking shape in Europe. "This will be the point of no-return for demand. We foresee an increase in the sales of electric cars by 2025 that will be 25% greater than our previous estimate, or 14.2 million vehicles accounting for 14% of the world market."

The Dutch bank ING sees things heading in the same direction. It predicts that electric cars will be dominant on Europe's roads (thus account for more than 50% of the market) by 2035. Its forecasts are based on, among other things, the public's readiness to embrace the Tesla Model 3 launched at the end of 2017 - now the best selling electric car in the U.S. - and Nissan's successful launch of its 2019 Leaf.

In its 2017 report, the financial analyst Bloomberg New Energy Finance (BNF) put the middle of the curve (50% mark) at 2040, whereas the 2016 report predicted that electric cars would account for only 35% of the market in 2040. The reasons that its analysts give for this adjustment are the main factors behind the creation of the "virtuous circle" that gives the S-curve its starting shape: the steadily declining prices of batteries, motors, and other components; the increasing production volumes; and the markedly longer lifespans of vehicles that are much simpler to make. BNF adds, "We see the curve's inflection point in the mid-2020s and sales to the tune of 3 million units in 2021 and accounting for about 5% of the European market and 4% of the Chinese market. Nevertheless, the public charging infrastructure will continue to call for sizable investments."

Even the most conservative analysts, such as OPEC's (Organization of Oil-producing Countries), are regularly revising their figures upwards! Their 2015 forecast was for electric vehicles accounting for 4% of new vehicle sales in 2040. Their forecast in 2016? 26% in 2040! Other oil company analyses, such as those of EXXON, Statoil, and BP, which cannot be accused of favoritism when it comes to electric vehicles, predict that at least 100 million electric cars will be sold between now and 2030 or 2035.

The major traditional automakers' CEOs' opinions swing between skepticism and resignation, but few, if any, of them are light-hearted about this breakthrough innovation. There are many reasons for this, but the main one is the companies' huge debt ratios. The billions of dollars that they have borrowed from the banks are guaranteed by the value of the plants that are used to manufacture their diesel engines and gearboxes!

So, in July 2017, the late Sergio Marchione, then big boss of Fiat-Chrysler, said, "We build cars, we sell them, and we manage to pay our bills. But I am not sure that we'll be able to make a profit from electrification. The answer must lie elsewhere, and the question is whether we are doing enough to find something else." Even more recently at the Detroit Auto Show in January 2018, we heard Jim Lentz, the big boss of Toyota North America, explain that it took Toyota 18 years to get a 3% market share with its hybrid, which is much less expensive than a 100% electric car. He thus very seriously feels that the electric car will end up getting 4-5% of the market, but "that is likely to take even much longer."

It should be noted, moreover, that most car makers have committed to "electrifying" their ranges. We have to interpret this message correctly and understand what it implies: It means adding something electric to their ranges. The new "electrified" models will be (sometimes plug-in) hybrids for the most part, but rarely electric cars without internal combustion engines, and the sentence "All our models will be electrified between now and 2022" that has been pronounced by Renault, Nissan, Mercedes, and other makers, means, "In four years' time there will be at least a hybrid version of each of our models" not "All our models will be electric only."

The Craig Station coal burning power plant in Colorado, USA, December 2011.

BY JIMMY THOMAS (IAGOARCHANGEL)

Winners and losers

Replacing internal combustion with electricity is a real breakthrough innovation that will transform the transportation and mobility of people radically the world over. While electricity suppliers and the installers of wind turbines and solar panels are overjoyed, the oil industry and combustion engine sector are potentially great losers. They are obviously trying to counter this development in order to limit their probable losses.

The first beneficiaries of the massive adoption of electric cars are the inhabitants of our major cities. They are being smothered by pollution, which has become one of the leading health problems in the world. Indeed, "urban canyons" slow down wind and prevent the dispersion of airborne pollutants, a large proportion of which comes from internal combustion engines. According to UNICEF, fine particles and nitrogen oxides are responsible for the early deaths of 500,000 people a year in Europe and probably five times as many in the major metropolises of Asia.

In the winner's corner we find the sectors that produce the raw materials used specifically to build electric cars, their motors, and their batteries, such as the miners and refiners of lithium, copper, nickel, cobalt, and other rare metals. It should be noted that half of these industries are in China.

The losers include fuel and lubricant distributors, but also the majority of car dealers and garages, the bulk of whose income comes from maintaining the complex mechanics of ICE cars, their exhaust systems, brakes, and gearboxes. Some service stations along major thoroughfares will avoid disaster by turning into shops, restaurants, and fast-food restaurants for the drivers who have to recharge their batteries during long trips, but most of them *will not* have this chance. Tire specialists should also survive, for the electric car's powerful acceleration is likely to be a gold mine for the tire business!

Oil distributors will ultimately have to cope with a dramatic fall in turnover and the almost complete disappearance of their service station networks. The makers of traditional cars, which are currently making huge profits on SUVs and big luxury sedans, are not taking kindly to the idea of turning their backs on decades of investment in the ICE. The automakers and subcontractors that do not make the right strategic choices in time will definitely lack the means to finance their transition. Consequently, we can expect an unprecedented wave of failures, restructuring, and mergers throughout the automotive sector.

Living with an electric car

Driving

Starting an electric car for the first time is surprising: You "turn the key in the ignition" and nothing happens, except for a light that goes on or a "ready" message displayed on the dashboard. Since there is no clutch, the car drives like an automatic: You accelerate with the pedal on the right and brake with the one on the left.

However, what really strikes you is the immediate, silent start. In ICE cars you hear the engine rev faster and faster, the gears catching, and then the more or less strong acceleration the next second. With an electric car, the car gets moving as soon as you graze the accelerator. There's no noise, no wait. It works and that's all! After a couple of hundred yards you'll notice that controlling your speed is much easier than with a gasoline engine. The right pedal alone modulates your speed very easily: you push down to go faster, and release it to slow down. You will say, "But that's how it works with my gas-powered car, too." However, an electric car always gives the same reaction for a given action, whereas accelerating and slowing down in a conventional car depend greatly on the engine speed: Flooring the accelerator will give very different effects if the engine is turning at 1,000 or 5,000 rpm. Releasing the accelerator likewise has a variable braking effect on the engine depending on the speed at which you are going and the engine's rpm.

This totally predictable way of operating is very reassuring, and given the lack of engine sounds, you discover that the car is a very pleasant way of getting about. A light touch on the radio's controls and the car is immediately filled with a soft musical atmosphere that doesn't have to be turned up to cover the purring engine sounds. Provided that you are behind the wheel of a recent electric vehicle with a decent driving range, your suburb-city commutes on clogged highways are a lot more relaxing than before. The lack of noise at low speeds and smooth operation reduce your level of stress and you'll be much more relaxed on arrival.

Curiously, riding in an electric car makes you much more aware of the noise and odors emitted by other vehicles. Remaining stuck in a traffic jam next to the exhaust pipe of a big diesel-engine four-wheel-drive vehicle quickly becomes very unpleasant.

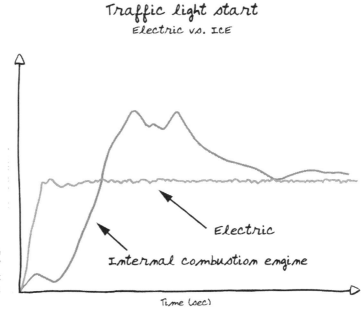

Traffic light start
Electric vs. ICE

Electric

Internal combustion engine

Acceleration at "ignition:" ICE vs electric motor.

Time (sec)

AVAS

In Europe, automakers whose cars are too quiet will gradually have to fit them (between 2019 and 2021) with an acoustic vehicle alert system (AVAS). This system will simulate the noise that an ICE makes from start-up to about 20 km/h (12,5 mi/h), including an increase in the volume with increasing speed.

Above 20 km/h, the driving sounds are deemed to be loud enough to warn non-motorized users that a vehicle is approaching. The driver will be able to switch the AVAS on and off.

The second thing that new drivers of electric vehicles discover is "one-pedal driving." Since you can modulate your speed very easily by the position of your right foot, you quickly realize that you no longer have to apply the brakes. In a descent or on approaching a bend or intersection, all you have to do is to lift your foot and the car slows down. After a few dozen miles, once you've got used to everything, your reflexes kick in and soon you'll be using the brake pedal only to go from a few miles per hour to a complete stop at a red light, in a traffic jam, or when you park the car. Unfortunately for their owners, some electric cars do not have a mechanism to regulate deceleration when you release the "gas" pedal. So, you still have to use the brakes for strong deceleration, such as stopping at the bottom of a hill. At the opposite end of the scale you have the Volkswagen e-Golf, which lets you choose from four levels of engine breaking, with Level 4 allowing real "One-Pedal Driving" that is very comfortable to use.

Simplicity and reliability

Unlike its fuel-burning sisters, the electric car comprises no elements that need to be warmed up to work. Its motor and transmission have more than 80% yields, which means that little energy is dissipated in the form of heat. With the internal combustion engine and its 30% yield, close to three-quarters of the energy used is turned into heat. And since the brakes are barely used in an electric car, they do not heat up a lot and show almost no wear. It is nothing out of the ordinary to check the brake pads of an electric car that has 120,000 mi (200,000 km) under its belt and find out that they do not yet need to be replaced.

An electric car comprises a score of moving parts compared with more than 2,000 in a gasoline-powered car. That's 99% fewer moving parts! What is more, the moving parts in an electric car simply revolve around themselves, without generating much heat. In contrast, hundreds of parts are constantly rubbing against each other in an ICE car, with most of these parts being bathed in oil to reduce wear and absorb the heat that is generated. The burning-hot combustion products that are given off by the engine are cooled in an exhaust system (the "muffler") in which highly corrosive high-temperature chemical reactions take place.

The electric motor: a single moving part.

The internal combustion engine: hundreds of moving parts.

A host of technical exploits were required to develop the precision mechanics of the modern engine. Yet, despite all that, hundreds of parts – the crankshaft, connecting rods, pistons, segments, valves, valve lifters, camshafts, injectors, gearbox dogs, belts, cooling circuit hoses, turbo-compressors, muffler, etc. - are subjected to rubbing and vibrations. And let's not forget the clutch. Even automatics have a clutch. The role of this little disk is to ease, by slipping, the process of getting the fixed parts (transmission and wheels) moving by connecting them to the engine (which cannot stop turning) when you start the car and each time you shift gears. The clutch is designed to wear down as slowly as possible, but it does a lot to improve the wages of a lot of garage mechanics!

So, to put it succinctly, the inevitable rubbing and heat generated in an ICE car mean that its lifespan is limited to about 120,000 mi (200,000 km). In contrast, the only parts that you can expect to undergo wear in an electric car are the tires and, to a lesser extent, the brake pads – all parts that are easy to replace. No mechanical part wears or gets hot for no purpose. An electric car thus has a very long lifespan. Of course, you must not forget to keep tabs on the ball bearings of the wheels and motor, but they are generally designed to last at least twenty years.

"And the battery?" That is the usual reaction to this unexpected discovery. The answer to the question is simple: Electric car batteries have a lifespan of several hundred thousand kilometers, but they are easy to replace in any event. Depending on the make, they may be provided under a rental agreement (and replaced when performance falls) or sold with a warranty, usually an 8-year warranty. We also see that the bigger the battery, the greater its range. Depending on the manufacturer, a battery reaches the end of its life when its capacity falls to 75 or 80% of its initial value. A battery's minimum lifespan is commonly estimated at between 120,000 and 180,000 mi (200,000–300,000 km). Since that is not immediately obvious, we shall look at battery life in greater detail in the next chapter.

The lifespans of lithium-ion batteries also depend, unfortunately, on their age. The capacity of an unused battery can drop considerable after some ten or so years if it remains idle for long periods of time. To minimize the risks during long months of inactivity, the battery must be left at a moderate temperature (between 40 and 70 °F / 5 and 20 °C) and charged at about 50%, i.e., the operating point where natural aging is felt the least. And, since an unused battery discharges slowly, you have to recharge the battery to this halfway mark after a few months to keep it in its optimal zone.

Given the lack of a long track record, it is difficult for us today to predict exactly how long a given battery will last. Indeed, its lifespan will depend not only on how little or intensively it is used, but also on its composition and storage and operating conditions. As a general rule, users consider the lifespan of an electric car battery to be better, even markedly better, in 2019 than what they initially expected. This is especially true for heavy users of electric vehicles, such as cab drivers and delivery van drivers in urban areas.

The lifespan of the rest of the vehicle is also much greater than that of a conventional car. That is because the mechanics contains much fewer parts and those parts are not subjected to heat or rubbing. What is more, to make it light, an electric car's chassis is made for the most part of sophisticated materials that are highly corrosion-resistant: aluminum, high-strength steel, even carbon fibers, as in the case of the BMW i3 and i8.

The lifespan of an electric car is generally put at 2½ times the lifespan of an ICE car, or 300,000 miles (500,000 km) (with a battery change at mid-life). Despite this obvious advantage, electric cars lose value each year according to the same depreciation tables as conventional cars because the used-car market does not yet have enough hindsight with regard to electric cars to be aware of this longevity difference and factor it into its equations. In contrast, vehicle fleet managers such as the post office and DHL based their decisions on the cost price per kilometer rather than the annual depreciation of their vehicles. And as soon as you divide the total of the purchase price plus maintenance costs by 500,000 instead of 200,000, the scales quickly tip in favor of electric solutions. In the U.S., there are more and more initiatives such as BlueLA, an all-electric car sharing service offering 200 charging points and 100 shared cars in Los Angeles with 24/7 access to self-service locations in the city centre. In Quebec, the Communauto car-sharing service is electrifing its fleet, which now has 120 electric vehicles. Its "no reservation" component in Montreal and Quebec City only offers hybrid or 100% electric vehicles.

No more filling up at the pump!

The routine of driving to the service station to fill up the tank disappears for electric car owners. It is replaced by connecting and disconnecting the charging plug at home. No more waiting at the pump or making a detour to find the cheapest gas in town; no more gasoline smell clinging to your clothes or fingers!

Slow charger for electric cars and hybrids on a street in the Netherlands.

And the cost of the electricity needed is a few pennies per kilometer covered, especially if you can benefit from a preferential off-peak rate.

That is where you realize that not all drivers have a garage or private parking lot in front of their home. How do you recharge the battery if you cannot do it at home? The electric car is not yet for everyone in 2019. If you do not have a parking spot with access to an electrical outlet, you're stuck! Of course, that is going to change quickly. The major urban centers have everything to gain if their residents switch to electric means of transport. However, to achieve that, cities will have to offer them a large number of "long-stay" parking spots with the possibility of recharging their cars.

The charging station logos have not yet been standardized across Europe, although the color green has been mainstreamed.

The city of London has understood this quite well and is starting to fit many of its central London street lights with recharging outlets. The corresponding parking spots are almost free for electric cars: *You pay 10 minutes on the meter and may stay as long as you want.* Londoners and many of the commuters who work in central London already enjoy the benefits of this innovation. The other major cities are observing London's experience before taking the plunge. We'll thus have to wait a few more years...

However, another solution is already being implemented, that of recharging at the workplace. Since electric cars are currently being used above all for commuting between home and work, enterprises located in downtown areas or on city outskirts that are mindful of their progressive image already offer specific parking places for employees who go electric.

The Dutch EV infrastructure provider Allego recently introduced a clever solution to meet this need, a patented system dubbed the "Charging Plaza." This is an effective solution for putting many charging outlets on the same parking lot. A central electric cabinet is connected to one, even several dozen, outlets spread around the parking lot. Charging is activated and paid for by means of a badge or an application that can be downloaded onto your smartphone. A Charging

Charging Plaza, an economically profitable wide-scale urban recharging solution.

Plaza makes it possible to charge many vehicles simultaneously at a maximum power of 43 kW AC, the central cabinet's task being to distribute the available energy among the cars "on line." You can also specify whether you want to recharge fully or just a few kilowatt-hours and if you are in a hurry to move on or willing to spend the night in the lot. The system allows for each hooked-up vehicle's needs and uses the available power as efficiently as possible without requiring that the existing infrastructure be upgraded. This type of "Smart Charging" is set to spread quickly and become the norm. Several Charging Plazas are already in service in Europe.

It is more and more clear that America's cities need to develop specific policies for the arrival of electric vehicles, create spaces for EV charging, rationalize parking rules, and support shared mobility and electric fleets.

Charging networks

Various power distribution grids designed specifically for electric cars have emerged these past few years. They include EVgo, Blink, ChargePoint, GreenLots, SemaConnect, OpConnect, Webasto, and several smaller operators in the USA.

With ChargePoint,
You Can Charge Three Ways

ChargePoint chargers are accessible via mobile app, smartwatch, or pass.

Circuit Électrique is the most extensive public recharging network in Canada. Plug In America, for its part, is a network that covers all of the Americas, from Santiago de Chile to Fairbanks, Alaska. These networks set up slow and quick charging stations in a wide variety of places from the street to the parking lots of government buildings, private companies, supermarkets, shopping malls, hotels, and restaurants. The charging points that are not free or government-subsidized can be accessed by a badge or a mobile phone application. Some require a monthly subscription, others do not.

The slow-charging stations have an available power of 3-22 kW, making it possible to recover from 6 to 60 miles (10 to 100 km) per hour of charging. The quick-charging stations provide 20-50 kW, and even up to 350 kW for some Ionity charging stations, and are well suited to stops on long

Charging station, not charger

Why do we talk about an EV charging station and not a charger? The battery of an electric vehicle is never recharged by connecting it to an external charger. The charging station thus is not a charger; it merely transmits a current (AC for slow charging, DC for quick-charging stations) from the grid to the car. If the charging station is public, it can also control access via a badge or magnetic card. The onboard electronics are what do the charging, that is, converting and measuring the exact amount of electrical current that is provided to charge the battery under the best conditions.

Public charging stations and home wall boxes are simple electrical outlets equipped with protective devices that send current to the battery when all safety conditions are met, for example, grounding with a differential switch to prevent electrocution or a circuit-breaker to protect from short-circuits.

trips. That is why they are often found at service stations or close to restaurants, snack bars, and other stopping places along major intercity routes, such as highway rest stops and on the outskirts of major cities.

The Tesla network

Tesla, the best-known EV brand in the world, offers what is probably the best solution to date, *i.e.*, a network of quick chargers dedicated exclusively to its cars. This network already covers all U.S. states, Canada, and Europe, and is distributed along the major thoroughfares to enable Tesla owners to leave the field of action of their own homes with short charging times, generally on the order of one hour. The network is distributed along all major interstate highways so Tesla owners can easily move to any location in North America.

In Canada, it is mainly deployed around Montreal and Vancouver, and the link between East Coast and West Coast, *via* Calgary and Winnipeg, should be operational by the end of 2020. With their 130 kW, the superchargers enable the Tesla S to cover another 156 miles (250 km) with just a twenty-minute charge.

An eight-car Tesla charging station in Rochester, NY (USA).

47

In addition to the quick-charging points, the Tesla network also includes hundreds of "destination charging stations." These are slower but located in places where the users stay longer, *e.g.*, hotels, restaurants, businesses, etc. They let you recoup "only" 60 miles (100 km) per hour of charging. There are more than 10,000 destination chargers in the United States, Europe and China. Tesla's North American network is expanding steadily, but Canada's central and maritime provinces remain the poor relations.

Between the cars' huge ranges and the make's extensive network of quick superchargers, Tesla owners are spoiled. They can drive long distances without the fear of "running out of juice," especially since the car's navigation screen automatically gives recommended routes that include the recharging breaks that are needed to reach your destination.

The other networks

ChargePoint. This network is the largest online network of independently-owned EV charging stations operating in 14 countries. Charging stations are activated with the ChargePoint card, a contactless credit card, or by using the associated mobile app. Prices are determined by the property owner. Many ChargePoint stations are free.

Semaconnect. Maryland-based SemaConnect offers Level 2 commercial grade EV charging stations and a management application called SemaCharge. SemaConnect stations are located in 20 U.S. states, including California and Washington, DC. The cost varies, as determined by the property owner.

Electrify America. In the aftermath of the Dieselgate scandal, the Volkswagen group was forced to invest 2 billion U.S. dollars in a charging network in the U.S. over ten years. This network was called "Electrify America." The network will have to include some quick-charging stations (150 kW) and even a certain number of superchargers capable of delivering 320 kW. Some of these stations were already open in the great metropolitan areas such as New York, Chicago, Seattle, and Washington, D.C., in 2017.

The Canadian subsidiary called "Electrify Canada" announced it is constructing 32 fast and ultra-fast charging stations in southern British Columbia, Ontario, and Quebec.

PetroCanada. PetroCanada announced in 2019 it is building a network of DC fast chargers from Halifax, Nova Scotia, to Vancouver, and every place in between. The ambition of PetroCanada is to compete directly with the coming Tesla link between East Coast and West Coast.

Flo and Circuit électrique. These two interconnected Canadian networks consist of more than 2,000 charging stations, with the bulk – 1,500 – including some 100 quick chargers, in Quebec. The Quebec network already makes it fairly easy to get around in EVs in the most densely populated parts of Quebec. In 2017 this network covered mostly Quebec, New Brunswick, and Eastern Ontario, but it is spreading quickly in Ontario and the Canadian West.

The most widespread networks in Quebec are Circuit électrique and Flo, but EVDuty, Sun Country Highway, Astria Technologies, and KsiNetwork (based in Ontario) are also present, along with ChargePoint and Blink Network, which cover all of North America. Lots of charging stations are being set up in Canada right now. Nova Scotia, for example, set up twelve new quick-charging stations that have made it possible to cover the entire province in an electric vehicle since spring 2018.

Ionity. In 2017 BMW, Daimler, Ford, and Volkswagen (with its subsidiaries Audi and Porsche) announced the creation of Ionity, a joint undertaking to develop an EV recharging network for long-distance travel across Europe. The Munich-based company plans to launch some 400 charging stations between now and 2020. A score were already open in Germany, Norway, and Austria in 2018. The most powerful charging stations in the Ionity network will be able to deliver up to 350 kW.

The occasional frustration

The occasional frustration crops up when one pulls into a charging station to find all the spots taken! Even worse is when they are taken by gas-powered cars that have simply found the spot more practical. If you park in the next spot in the row you are very close to the charger, but of course the cable is 4" too short to connect! According to the rules of fair play, charging station spots should be occupied only by charging electric cars and each owner should disconnect her/his car and free up the space as soon as additional charging is not needed. In most countries, the "EV charging spot" signs are informative only. They have no binding force and have not been formally included in the traffic code or legislation. That means you have no legal recourse against inconsiderate drivers; you must simply hope that courteousness will quickly become customary!

Unfortunately, the electric car has become the victim of its success. In Los Angeles and Oslo we have already witnessed some exemplary cases of "charge rage" with drivers in need of a quick fix at loggerheads with charging spot squatters. To get its users to behave correctly, the Tesla network recently added a supplement for connect time without charging.

The rules of etiquette at charging spots all derive from common sense: If you hesitate as to whether a charging station is private or public, ask! Never block a charging spot if you do not have to charge your battery. If you foresee having to leave your car to charge over a long period of time, leave a note on the dash board explaining how to get in touch with you.

There is, however, an exception to this rule: In the case of charging stations located in airport parking lots it is difficult to take a driver to task for taking up a spot, as the driver is surely gone for several hours or even days. In such cases, the rule "first come, first served" applies. Still, we can hope that airports are aware of the problem and will quickly increase the number of charging stations at our disposal.

The take-home message? "I've finished charging, so I free the spot."

Driving range

The distance that an electric car can cover is the main worry of future EV owners. This is completely understandable, given the tiny ranges provided by the first electric vehicles put on the market. Luckily, the rapid advances made in lithium battery prices and capacity opened the door to the "second generation," represented since 2017 by the Nissan Leaf 30 kW/40 kW, Chevrolet Bolt, and Tesla Model 3, which all have a minimum range of 120 mi (200 km) under real conditions of use. With these cars and the networks of rapid chargers that are being deployed, the risks of running out of power are becoming more subsidiary.

Since we are still in the first part of the S-curve of EV adoption, almost all of these cars are bought as the second car in two-car families. That means that they will be used mainly for local driving and daily commutes between home and work. Of course, they can still be used for long trips, but the disadvantages of having to recharge along the way are no longer decisive if you have to deal with them on an exceptional basis. Taking a 20- or 30-minute break every 120 to 180 miles (200 to 300 km) is acceptable when you take such trips just a few times a year.

Choosing the right battery

"Driving range anxiety" disappears if the car has been chosen wisely from the very start. Indeed, if you never drive long distances, you might as well choose the cheapest car with its

---

Kilowatt-hours and miles

The amount of energy stored in a battery is expressed in kilowatt-hours (kWh). One kilowatt-hour corresponds to the power of 1 kilowatt (1,000 watts) for 1 hour. Each kilowatt-hour lets you drive between 2.4 and 5.4 miles (4 and 9 kilometers), depending on the vehicle.

The most efficient cars – the VW e-up! and Hyundai Ioniq – manage to go 5.6 mi (9 km) with a single kilowatt-hour. The least efficient, but also the heaviest and most luxurious models – the Tesla S and X – cover just a little over 2.4 mi (4 km) with the same power consumption. However, their batteries are three or four times bigger, which largely offsets this disadvantage.

small battery. Even if you occasionally need a greater range, carrying around a larger, heavier, and more expensive battery all the time is not very efficient, since the car will use more power all year round against only one advantage: gaining a few minutes of charging time along the way a few days in the year when you have to take a long trip. In such a scenario, it is better to choose a car that can be recharged very quickly rather than one that has a huge battery.

Manufacturers and car magazines put the range forward as the number-one criterion for choosing a battery, but they all overlook the common-sense argument of requiring quick charges to meet the problem of occasional long-distance travel.

In 1% of the cases...

automakers are cognizant of the limitations created by their cars' limited mileage and propose various solutions: Tesla has its own network of superchargers that solves 99% of the problems "painlessly." However, since the price of a Tesla makes this network inaccessible for most of us, others are circumventing the problem. Nissan, for example, proposes a "mobility pack" with the purchase of a Leaf in Europe. The aim of this pack is to facilitate long-distance travel with special conditions for renting a car. The buyer gets a card that is valid for three years and points that can be exchanged for a free car hire of up to four weeks good for all ICE vehicles at Hertz.

Understanding range

"Driving range anxiety" exists above all in the minds of future electric car owners. Once they become users and habits take root, this anxiety is replaced by "range awareness." Knowledge of where the charging spots are located along known routes of travel quickly leads to a certain peace of mind. The reasoning is as follows: "If I get as far as X, I'll be able to recharge and thus get back home." However, the main source of reassurance is awareness of how the battery works. When the way something works becomes foreseeable, it is no longer frightening. Still, we must admit that the behavior of an electric car's energy gauge is surprising at the start.

All electric vehicles are designed to give the driver as much information as possible about the charge remaining in the battery, usually expressed in kilometers or miles of travel, and the best way to use the available energy. Thanks to this information, you quickly realize the importance of three factors that conventional car drivers never worry about, namely, speed, altitude, and temperature.

Let's look first at the first two of these factors, *i.e.*, speed and altitude, which are nothing more than two forms of energy available for an electric vehicle.

The distance that a car can still cover at a given moment depends directly on the amount of energy that is available in the battery to run the motor. However, we tend to overlook the two other forms of energy that are also available, that is, kinetic energy and potential energy, simply because these two forms of energy are not reusable in the case of ICE cars. Kinetic energy is the energy stored by a car when it is moving, whereas potential energy is the energy produced by the forces of gravity.

In a nutshell, we can say that

Usable Energy = battery's E + kinetic E + potential E

where:

Usable Energy = energy that can be used at a given moment.

Battery's E = energy remaining in the battery.

Kinetic E = energy due to movement. It is zero when an object is stationary and increases with the square of velocity.

Potential E = energy due to gravity. It is zero at sea level and increases with increasing elevation.

Kinetic energy

Accelerating consumes energy, then, once a constant speed is reached, just enough energy is consumed to offset the losses due to friction on the ground and in the air. However, when the electric car stops, it recovers its energy of movement – its kinetic energy – and returns it to the battery. In cars with gasoline engines, this energy is not recovered and is dissipated as heat in the brakes. The kinetic energy varies with the vehicle's mass and the square of its speed. It is put at

Hybrid cars use kinetic energy recovery to increase their driving ranges. That enables them to reduce their fuel consumption since, while the gasoline engine is still used to accelerate, the deceleration phases are used to charge the battery, which will help the gasoline engine in turn and thus lower its mean consumption.

some 1 mile of driving range for a 5,500 lb (2,500 kg) vehicle moving at 60 mph (100 km/h). However, since it varies with the square of the velocity, it quickly rises in magnitude, to 2 miles for a speed of 85 mph and 4 miles for a speed of 120 mph.

In practice, accelerating from a standstill to a normal high-way speed reduces the car's range by about 1.2 mile. However, electric cars recover their kinetic energy when they decelerate, so if you slow down until you come to a stop, that energy is recovered and returned to the battery. That is the theory. In realty, that is not exactly what happens, because the motor, transmission, and electronic control circuit do not have yields of 100%. Nevertheless, the general consensus is that between 70 and 80% of the energy used to accelerate is recovered on slowing down.

Potential energy

Now for the role of gravity. If you start at the summit of a mountain, you will have no need of fuel to cover great distances. As long as you go downhill, no effort is needed. Those who have already pushed a car to get it started understand very well where the problem lies! Potential energy is used very simply, without your having to think about it. With a conventional car, we do not really think about the fact that we have to push down harder on the accelerator going up and less going down a slope. We know full well that the car will use more gas up a hill, but we do not really pay attention to that.

Yet when drivers go their first few miles in an electric car they tend to worry when they see the first major ups and downs. With an energy meter marked in units of distance, the importance of potential energy becomes obvious. And indeed,

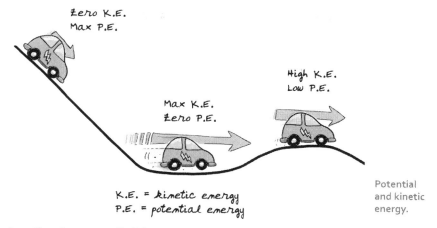

Zero K.E.
Max P.E.

High K.E.
Low P.E.

Max K.E.
Zero P.E.

K.E. = kinetic energy
P.E. = potential energy

Potential and kinetic energy.

its effect is not negligible: It is calculated that with an average car weighing 5,550 lb (2,500 kg), about 1 mile of range will be used for each 30 to 40 feet' increase in elevation. So, climbing out of a valley to a 1000-feet higher elevation decreases the range by about thirty miles. Hence the reaction, "But driving uphill uses up a huge amount of energy!" Yes, that is true! But since we are talking about an electric car, the return trip will not be driven free-wheeling or braking with the engine, as one does with a conventional car. On the contrary, the energy recovery mechanism works perfectly well and here, too, recovers about three-quarters of the energy consumed climbing. That means that once it is back at its starting point, our electric car will have recovered some ten or so miles of driving range and, in the final analysis, the net result will be fairly close to that of driving on the flat.

Temperature

Lithium batteries are complex devices in which charging and discharging are linked to chemical reactions. As all chemists will tell you, temperature influences reaction speed and yields greatly. High temperatures – more than 122 °F (50 °C) – are harmful to batteries. If they are used at such temperatures, they are more fragile and age faster. The very functioning of the batteries generates a certain amount of heat, called "losses from internal resistance," and the heat generated during charging and discharging causes the temperature to rise. That is why air or liquid cooling devices are foreseen in electric vehicles. They automatically keep the temperature below a reasonable threshold and can sometimes be heard even when the vehicle is at a standstill. That will often be the case, for example, during quick charging with a supercharger.

The temperature range that is considered acceptable for an EV battery is between 5 and 115 °F (-15 °C to 45 °C). The manufacturers nevertheless warn that the battery's capacity can fall significantly at temperatures below freezing. If you live or drive in cold regions, such as Quebec, Alaska, or Scandinavia, electric car dealers will probably recommend that you adopt one or the other solution to minimize the problems entailed by freezing temperatures. There are two main options, which can be combined, moreover: insulate the battery and thus the floor of the vehicle or add an active battery heating unit, such as the ZHV option for the BMW i3. The second option will use a few dozen watts, but the enhanced battery yield can make it worthwhile. Even if, in extreme cases, such as when it is -20 °F outside, the electric car loses half of its driving range, it is still very reassuring to know that it will start immediately, without a hitch, whereas in the case of a gasoline ICE, problems starting up are legion in very cold weather, never mind the inconvenience of the time necessary for the engine to warm up to a decent temperature.

Charging a lithium battery in freezing temperatures can be detrimental to its lifespan. Luckily, the chargers are designed either to preheat the battery or to start charging slowly so that the battery's high internal resistance warms the battery slowly (or faster if it has been well insulated from the cold), and charging *per se* can truly start only once the battery has been warmed up. Since the car is equipped with an automatic battery cooling system, you don't have to be afraid of it overheating. The only inconvenience for the user will be that charging will take more time than at more clement temperatures.

When conditions are not extreme – let's say, in the 30-80 °F / 0-25 °C range – the temperature nevertheless influences the battery's capacity. The rated value of a battery that is given by

its manufacturer assumes that the battery is at "room temperature," a term that is not always clearly defined but can be
assumed to be 70 °F. As soon as the temperature drops below
this reference temperature, the battery's capacity drops, for
the chemical reactions involved slow down. A battery is generally thought to lose around 0.7% of its capacity for a 1 °F
drop in temperature. So, at 32 °F (0 °C), the battery will have
lost 25% of its baseline capacity and the driving range of a
fully-charged car will be reduced proportionately with respect
to the manufacturer's figures. Still, don't panic! As soon as
the temperature rises again, the capacity will rise, too. The
energy contained in a cool battery does not disappear; it
simply becomes temporarily inaccessible.

Optimizing range

Just as with a diesel or gas engine, your driving style strongly
influences the mileage you get with an electric car. As we've
seen above, its range at a given point in time results from
the context. But how can the battery's available capacity be
used most efficiently? Everything depends on the circumstances. Many parameters are at play in any vehicle's energy
consumption, but the main ones are as follows:

- rolling resistance (friction),
  which depends on the weight and tires;
- aerodynamic resistance (drag),
  which depends on the vehicle's shape and speed;
- the use of accessories,
  mainly heating and air conditioning; and
- driving style: acceleration and braking.

The bulk of the time you have absolutely no need to pay attention to all these parameters. If you are not planning to take
long trips that are out of the ordinary, keeping tabs on your
consumption is not very important. After all, an electric car
is very cheap to run, in terms of cost per unit distance, even
with the heating on full blast and the radio blaring! However,
if you've decided to make a trip in an electric car for your

vacation, you will definitely want to optimize your range every way possible.

Rolling resistance. The mechanical yield of a car is never 100%. Even though electric motors perform much better than internal combustion engines, various speed-reducing phenomena exist in all vehicles, regardless of the means of propulsion. The most important ones are the movements of the suspension and rubbing of the tires on the road. That is why electric cars have stiff suspensions and their tires are narrow and molded in low-rolling-resistance rubber.

The vehicle's weight crushes the springs of the suspension with each bump in the road and compresses the rubber of the tires, causing them to heat up, with each turn of the wheel. To minimize energy loss, the driver has but two options: make sure that the tires are always well inflated and never carry unnecessary weight. For example, taking fifty pounds out of the trunk will let you cover an additional 1% of distance.

Air resistance. The faster a car moves, the more the air will slow its progress. The aerodynamic resistance of a car depends on three factors: its speed, frontal surface area, and shape. The shape coefficent (Cx) depends on the outer silhouette but also on all the passages that let air into the car.

©MotorBlog.com

The Volkswagen XL1's shape enables it to achieve a Cx of 0.186.

Cx

The Cx of an object is its drag coefficient. This figure represents the object's ability to penetrate the air more or less easily, with 1 equal to the coefficient of a cube in movement and 0 an object that would not be hampered at all by the air as it advanced. A Cx of 0.3 is normal for a passenger car.

The Volkswagen XL1 almost-prototype of 2014 is probably the world champion of aerodynamics. It achieved a Cx of 0.186 in exchange for a few compromises: neither radiator grill nor side mirrors and rear wheels embedded in the body. Volkswagen sold 200 units at more than €100,000 (US$120,000, CAN$155,000) apiece!

If we look at the electric cars that are actually available on the market, the Tesla Model 3 and Model S stand out with Cx values of 0.21 and 0.24, respectively. In comparison, the best gas-powered cars are the Jaguar XE, Mazda 3, and Audi A6, which are all tied with a Cx of 0.26. The hybrid BMW i8 also achieves this figure.

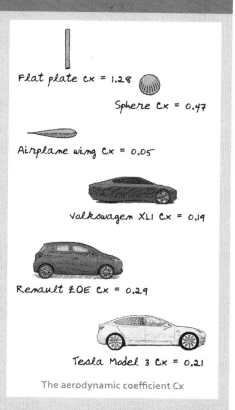

Flat plate cx = 1.28

Sphere cx = 0.47

Airplane wing cx = 0.05

Volkswagen XL1 cx = 0.19

Renault ZOE cx = 0.29

Tesla Model 3 cx = 0.21

The aerodynamic coefficient Cx

Because of their compact shapes, the small electric cars designed for city driving have less favorable aerodynamic profiles, but their calling is not hours of fast highway driving. So, the French Renault has a Cx of 0.29 while the Cx of the Volkswagen e-up! does not drop below 0.31.

The bottom of an electric car is smooth and its shape is not affected by the presence of an exhaust pipe and muffler. Its overall silhouette is streamlined to reduce drag and it does not need a big radiator, such as ICE cars do, or huge openings to cool down the brakes. Air flows inside the body are reduced, which means that electric cars always have better Cx values than their fuel-burning counterparts. To improve things even more, the air vents for cooling the motor and battery are often closed by motorized valves that open only when necessary and the wheels have practically completely smooth rim flaps. Consequently, their Cx values are often below 0.3.

Size also contributes to drag. So, to compare two vehicles, you have to compare not only their Cx values, but their SCx values as well, SCx being the product of the car's frontal area times its shape coefficient.

Drag is dependent on the square of the velocity. That means that simply because of air resistance, driving at 60 mph instead of 30 mph uses four times rather than twice the energy! Cars with low SCx values thus have a great advantage on the highway. On the other hand, the aerodynamic criterion is much less important for small urban models, which rarely exceed speeds of 50 mph (80 km/h).

The main thing to remember from this discussion of aerodynamics is that driving fast costs a pretty penny in mileage! A drive in the suburbs in which you are at 30 mph half the time and 60 mph the other half will use up 15-20% more

Following a truck

The journalist Andy Miles tested the performance of his Peugeot iOn – a not-very-streamlined city compact – at 60 mph (100 km/h) on a highway and compared its energy consumption when he kept it close behind a car, a bus, or a large truck. He was able to drive 20% farther if he played "follow the leader." When he repeated the same trip at 67 mph without following a truck, his car's driving range fell 12%. This experiment confirms the importance of aerodynamics on a car's mileage.

Warning: If you want to test this driving strategy, remain vigilant! A truck may brake at any time for reasons that you cannot see if you are following close behind.

energy than the same trip performed at a constant intermediate speed. So, it is better to make a long trip at a constant speed of 50 mph than to alternate between slow and very fast zones. You can also improve your mileage by avoiding highways and preferring state or national roads. In some cases, losing a few minutes on the journey may be very worthwhile if this enables you to reach your destination without having to stop for a recharge.

Accessories. Air-conditioning and heating use huge amounts of electricity. To reduce such energy expenditures, many electric cars use a heat pump to produce warm air. Some of them, such as the Nissan Leaf, use a reversible pump that can produce heat or cold and use less energy than a traditional air-conditioning compressor. Depending on the manufacturer's technological choices and volume to heat up or cool down, air-conditioning and heating use between one and three kilowatts, thereby reducing the vehicle's driving range commensurately.

Heating tip. Many electric cars, such as the Tesla, Nissan, Volkswagen, and Renault, give you the possibility of pre-heating (or cooling) the passenger area before starting, *i.e.*, when the car is still plugged into the charger. This option is very interesting, especially for short trips, for, thanks to the preheating, you avoid the huge drain on the battery that turning on the heater entails.

The preheater can be programmed ahead of time or switched on as required, as is the case for launching or stopping charging. The methods vary from one brand to the next, but as a rule, a mobile phone application is used. Some prefer to use a remote controller, the onboard computer's screen, or a specific Internet portal such as ConnectedDrive for BMW owners or Car-Net for Volkswagens.

Preheating is really very interesting for residents of very cold regions, especially if it can be coupled to preheating the battery. When the outside temperatures are very low, preheating the battery will increase the battery's capacity by a few percent.

Heated seats and steering wheels are a fairly useless luxury in an ICE car, where more than half of the energy from the fuel is turned into heat and available for heating the interior. In contrast, there is no free source of heat in an electric car. So, it is sometimes more worthwhile to switch on the seat warmer while keeping the interior heating to a minimum. You will use much less electricity than if you heat the entire interior for an almost identical feeling of comfort, unless the outside temperature is too bitterly cold. Unlike space heating, the seat warmers use only a few dozen watts and do not reduce the car's driving range noticeably.

The small accessories such as radio, interior lights, and fan have negligible energy consumption and thus do not affect the driving range. As for the head- and taillights, not switching them on when necessary is out of the question. You are not going to put yourself in danger to save electricity. In any event, the power absorbed by all of the outside lights of a car rarely exceeds 200 watts, meaning that they will reduce the car's range by barely more than 1%.

To increase the car's range, it is possible, weather permitting, to switch off the heating or air-conditioning or at least reduce its consumption by adjusting the thermostat. Most automakers propose an energy-saving "Eco mode" that disconnects the energy-intensive accessories and limits the motor's power. This is a simple way to extend the car's mileage by some twenty percent or so.

Driving style. The driving style puts all the elements that we have just mentioned into play. You learn how to drive economically rather quickly. Moreover, you are helped by various visual signals. The methods and names vary from one make to the next, but the general idea is to display an "ecodriving score" that is easy to keep high by driving smoothly. As a rule, driving at a constant speed and foreseeing the need to slow down in order to give the battery enough time to recover energy will maximize the available driving range. In city traffic, energy consumption remains very small because of the low average speed, despite the frequency of accelerations and decelerations. Outside the city, however, everything depends on the mean speed because of aerodynamic braking, which is preponderant over 50 mph. Main roads are thus advisable, if your route allows you to avoid high-speed segments (highways) without penalizing the mean speed too much. And when it comes to long trips, staying some 6 mph (10 km/h) below the speed limit will not cost a lot of time but could save you up to 10% on your mileage, especially for cars with high Cx values, such as the small city cars.

Record hunters will advise you to protect your car from headwinds by driving behind a truck or at a constant very slow speed. However, in practice, it is better to adopt a relaxing and relaxed driving style for long trips (moreover, the lack of engine sounds will be conducive to that) and take advantage of the recharging breaks with places equipped with rapid chargers to rest or have a bite to eat.

Recharging fully or not?

Should you always charge your battery fully? Why not if you have a charger at home, a full night ahead, and a reduced off-peak electricity rate? Having a battery that is always fully charged to be ready for all situations seems to be a good idea. But, things are more complex than they seem at first glance.

For example, if you live in a mountain village, why charge your battery to the hilt before dropping 1000 feet in elevation at the start of each trip? The effect of gravity could easily add the capacity to cover a few dozen kilometers more in the first

A good quick recharge with cables for the three types of
connection used in Europe: (from left to right) Type 2, CCS Combo, and ChaDeMo.

few minutes of travel. However, if the battery is fully charged
at the start, not only are you going to miss an opportunity to
recharge free of charge, but in addition you will be forced to
slow the car by braking. In such a case, you would do better to
charge up to 90% of the maximum charge and not wear down
your brake pads as you descend into the valley! In contrast,
if you live at the seaside or in a valley, don't hesitate to make
sure that your battery is fully charged and heat the interior
if it is cold outside. Charging the battery fully is not harmful,
for the onboard charge controller will ensure that the battery
always stays within its allowed operating range and the battery's longevity will not be affected by the charging conditions.

Nor is it interesting to charge your battery fully when
fast-charging on a long trip. The fast chargers supply 50 kW,
or even more, for charging, but this is the actual power for
between only 10 and 80% of the charge level. Indeed, when
the battery's voltage rises and approaches its maximum, the
current delivered by the charger falls little by little and the
charging slows down. And this does not allow for the fact
that as the battery warms up under the effects of the fast

charging, the car's charge-control electronics will start to limit the current to prevent overheating. In a word, charging to restore the last twenty percent of the battery's capacity is likely to take longer than expected. It is thus probably wiser to get back on the road and plan your next stop rather than waiting what seem like never-ending minutes to reach the 100% mark. And of course, if you are approaching your final destination, planning a safety margin of a few dozen kilometers will suffice. There is no need to reach a destination equipped with a charging station with a half-full battery!

Recharging and battery life: If you are particularly mindful about preserving your battery's life, it may be worthwhile to program a charging cutoff at 90% of capacity for daily recharging and charge fully (to 100% of capacity) only when a long trip is foreseen. Of course, this is possible only if your vehicle's computer offers this option. Charging the battery 100% is not detrimental to the battery; rather, the harm comes from leaving the battery fully charged for too long, especially in very warm weather. Harmful irreversible chemical reactions can occur in lithium batteries, but they are worrisome only when the three parameters "heat, charge, and duration" are at their maximum limits. This desire to preserve battery life is also an argument for buying the biggest battery possible, for the need to charge up fully will be less frequent with a powerful battery.

Pollution and a good ecological conscience

In 2019 we are living in the first stages of the S-curve of EV adoption and being powered by electricity when you drive will make you an "innovator" or "early adopter." This feeling of having made the right choice before the crowd is reassuring.

Solar panels and electric cars

One-third of electric car owners in the USA generate at least part of their electricity with photovoltaic panels, which obviously improves their CO_2 budgets.

Whereas in 2010 and 2012 the very first innovators of the "zero emissions" vehicle sometimes wondered whether they had made a well-founded choice, this doubt has now been completely dispelled, for electric vehicles are less polluting and generate smaller amounts of greenhouse gases than their ICE equivalents. While this was not 100% certain ten years ago, it can now be proven scientifically, even in countries such as Poland, where the bulk of the country's electricity is generated by coal-fired plants: Over its entire lifespan, from mining the metal ores to end-of-life (EOL) recycling, with its consumption in between, the electric car contributes half as much to global warming as a conventional gas- or diesel-powered car. With the growth of renewables, the beneficial influence of electric propulsion on climate change mitigation will continue to increase.

Participating, however little, in controlling global warming and reducing air, water, and soil pollution are useful for society but also reinforce the feeling of personal well-being. All those little instants when, stuck in a traffic jam in a tunnel, you realize that you are driving one of the rare vehicles that are not contributing to making the air a poisonous miasma, or when you drive by a gas station without having to stop, are good for your morale. This good ecological conscience comes across very often in social network messages and helps to promote the "electric car" phenomenon indirectly.

Cost price

The automobile market is oriented much more by the sales prices of cars than by their running costs (cost per km or mile). If the opposite were true, there would probably be many more electric vehicles on the road. This is because the major strength of electric propulsion is its low cost price per unit distance. In 2019 we shall still be in the very first phases of adopting a new technology in the throes of development. Make no mistake about it: We can expect to see the sales prices of electric cars fall in the coming years.

The major guidelines are already in place: An electric car is at least two to three times as robust and durable as a much more complex ICE car and the batteries have a manufacturer-guaranteed 6- or 8-year lifespan and maintain their performance levels for at least 2,000 charging cycles, which corresponds to 250,000 miles for a car with a 125-mile range! Given energy consumption reduced to one-third of

Costs per mile

TCO

The *total cost of ownership* of a car over its lifespan, or TCO, consists of three parts: the initial price (of the purchase or leasing arrangement minus possible subsidies), annual costs (taxes, insurance, motor vehicle inspections, CO_2 contribution, and subscriptions), and the cost per mile (energy used, highway tolls, tire and brake wear). The problem with the TCO is that it is not known until afterwards, at the end of the vehicle's life.

ECU

Before buying a car, fleet operators estimate the costs over four years, which is the typical length of time that a vehicle is kept in a fleet, after which it is sold on the used-car market. They then compute the year-by-year cost by calculating the difference in value between the start and the end of each year and then adding up the figures for the four years. This is referred to as the *Estimated Cost of Use* or ECU. The difference between TCO and ECU can be as large as 20%.

CPM

The *cost price per mile* or CPM is the total cost of ownership over the car's lifespan divided by the number of miles covered. As one can easily understand, this cost per mile depends on the number of miles driven per year.

a conventional car's and reduced maintenance costs, it is easy to understand that even the currently high purchase price will be offset by the lower running costs at some time in the course of the vehicle's life. That means that we should ultimately see a shift in behavior and a significant increase in the prices of second-hand electric cars.

The low actual price of each mile driven is appreciated in particular by the managers of fleets of vehicles that are driven a lot, as in major distribution and transportation companies. So, it comes as no surprise to find mail services and parcel delivery companies such as DHL, as well as car-sharing fleets in large cities, among the first companies to jump on the electric car bandwagon.

Expenditures on energy and maintenance are much lower in the case of electric vehicles than conventional vehicles. In contrast, their purchase prices are higher. So, there is nothing astonishing about the fact that the best-ranked elec-

Energy cost comparison

According to standardized EPA consumption figures, an electric vehicle uses between 25 and 32 kWh to go 100 miles (160 km). At the U.S. average cost of 14 cents/kWh, the electric mile thus costs between 3.50 and 4.50 cents.

Still according to the Environmental Protection Agency, an average ICE vehicle has a fuel economy of 25 miles per gallon. In the USA, with diesel at $3.00 per gallon and gasoline at $2.30 per gallon, running on these fossil fuels costs 12 cents/mi for diesel and 9.2 cents for gas.

A study by Michigan's Transport Research Institute asserted in January 2018 that the energy costs of new electric cars were below those of their new ICE equivalents in every state in the Union and were on average 56% cheaper for the U.S. as a whole, including in Hawaii, where electricity cost goes as high as 33 cents/kWh.

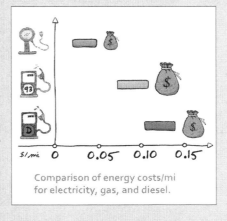

Comparison of energy costs/mi for electricity, gas, and diesel.

tric cars according to cost cer mile (CPM) are the small city models, which are among the cheapest on the market and use little energy thanks to their small motors and low mean speeds in city traffic.

In Europe, the CPM of an electric car in 2019 is still higher than that of an equivalent ICE car if it covers less than 120,000 miles in its lifetime. Beyond this threshold the CPM becomes more interesting, but the actual figures vary with the country and its tax incentives and electricity rates.

The typical electric car resale value after five or ten years is difficult to predict, but we can suppose that the market will continue to model its depreciation after that of ICE cars for several more years, meaning that its price will not be very high, either.

The high initial purchase price remains the main hurdle in buying an electric car. So, buying a used electric car can be an excellent deal. Let's not forget that the lifespan of an electric car is two to three times greater than that of a gas-powered car. A second-hand Kia Soul EV (4 years old, 40,000 miles on the clock) that is bought for $12,000 will have usually exactly the same warranty as a new car and be just as reliable, with a remaining lifespan of more than 120,000 mi. So, if you live in a state, country, or region where EV purchases are not heavily subsidized, pore over the classifieds on the other side of the border, for owners who sell subsidized vehicles take the subsidy into account in calculating their asking prices and will pass on a large portion of the advantage that they got to you.

Indeed, we are starting to see garages specialized in second-hand electric cars popping up and they will be in a good position to help you make the right choice. In conclusion, if we do the computation over 4-5 years, the cost price per mile of a new electric car in 2019 will be interesting maybe in 50% of cases, those corresponding to above-average annual mileage or special circumstances, such as special access to

One of the rare second-hand EV dealers – Simon André in Trois-Rivières, Quebec.

free charging stations. Nevertheless, the differences in the CPM of electric cars and those with gasoline engines are not very high. Despite the variability of fuel prices and tax incentives between regions, electric cars never cost more than 20% more per mile than ICE cars in the most unfavorable cases. On the other hand, if we calculate the CPM over a more realistic lifespan of 10-15 years, the figures tilt in favor of electric cars 80% of the time. So, in 2019, buyers who are mindful of cost-effectiveness will have two options: either buy a new electric car with a view to keeping it for a long time, or take advantage of the used-car market's current underestimation of a used EV's value and buy a recent used model.

It should also be noted that the total cost per mile in 2020 will be lower than that in 2019, which is already lower than the CPM in 2018. In response to rising ranges and falling battery prices, we expect the CPM to continue to fall steadily for several more years.

How
does it work?

In this chapter, readers who want to learn more about the way an electric car and its main components, such as the motor and battery, work will get detailed answers to their questions.

This book is not an electrotechnics manual. However, few drivers know how the main basic components of an electric car work, whereas they have been bathed in an internal combustion engine culture for more than 100 years and are familiar with the basic vocabulary: pistons, cylinders, clutch, muffler, oil filter, and so on. We shall thus demystify the key words of the 21st-century car aficionado: induction motor, lithium battery, supercharger, and a few more. To streamline the text, the meanings of the main technical terms are given in the glossary at the end of the book.

General architecture

First-generation electric cars are merely adaptations of existing models to which a battery has been added and the ICE replaced by an electric motor. The Ford Focus Electric, VW e-Golf, Smart ForTwo electric drive, and Kia Soul EV belong to this category. Not until the new generations, designed from the start with the idea of electric propulsion only, have the advantages of electricity been used fully. The BMW i3, Volkswagen's future I.D. range, the Jaguar i-Pace, and all the Tesla models already have an architecture designed for electricity from the get-go. The main shared characteristic of these new cars is to incorporate the battery in the floor to lower the car's center of gravity and free up a maximum amount of space for the occupants and baggage.

The motor-transmission unit of an electric car is five times more compact than that of a conventional car. The motor itself is very compact: 640 to 1280 cubic inches suffices to house a 100 hp electric motor. Since the motor-stepdown transformer-differential unit does not have to be connected to a cumbersome exhaust system, it can be nestled in the bottom of the space between the rear wheels.

The Volkswagen MEB, a basic platform designed from the start for the electric car. Here, a four-wheel-drive configuration with two motors.

In the first-generation electric cars that use an existing front-wheel-drive platform, such as the e-Golf, the motor-transmission group takes the place of the ICE and its gearbox. This arrangement is less efficient and requires the addition of transmission rods to enable the front wheels to turn. On the other hand, it makes it possible to take advantage of a cheap existing platform that is manufactured in large series.

Attention!

As soon as you open the hood of an electric car your attention will be drawn to a series of fairly large-caliber orange cables. These are the power cables, and they can constantly be carrying potentials of 200-600 volts, even when the ignition is off. In some vehicles, other bright yellow or fluorescent blue cables are also at high voltage. So, you should be very careful with regard to all colored cables. In electric cars, all orange cables are dangerous, but they may not be the only hazardous cables!

In all cases, it is better to leave the maintenance of an electric vehicle to technicians with safety training. They wear Class 00 gloves that protect them from voltages of up to 1,000 V and know how to disconnect the battery safely.

Danger: Orange cables are at high voltage!

Never touch or disconnect orange cables!

The high-end electric cars that offer four-wheel drive use two separate motors, one in front and the other at the rear. The front motor generates additional power and makes the vehicle more agile, but the main motor remains housed between the rear wheels. The front motor is compact enough to leave room for a trunk under the hood. The four-wheel-drive two-motor arrangement has the additional advantage of recovering the energy of deceleration more effectively because the weight of the vehicle shifts onto the front wheels when the brakes are applied.

The motor

There are two types of electric motor for cars, the induction motor and the permanent-magnet motor, each with its advantages and drawbacks. Their architectures are very similar and composed of two parts: The fixed part or stator is a hollow cylinder with three windings of copper wire lodged in its thickness. The mobile part or rotor turns on its axis inside the stator. The rotor is supported by two ball bearings. So, an electric motor contains only one mobile part. That explains its great robustness.

The electronics module injects strong currents one at a time into each of the three windings of the stator, thereby creating a turning magnetic field. This magnetic field will entrain the rotor in its wake, which creates the driving force that moves the vehicle forward. Despite the motor's very good yield, the stator nevertheless heats up. It must thus be cooled down with a fluid that also serves to regulate the battery's temperature.

The difference between the two types of motor lies in the rotor. In the permanent-magnet motor, the rotor is a set of powerful magnets embedded in a stack of iron sheets. The magnets are attracted by the turning magnetic field generated by the stator and entrain the motor's axle.

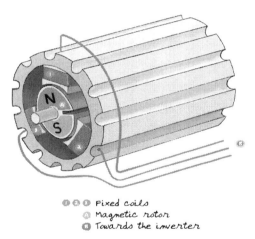

● ● ● Fixed coils
● Magnetic rotor
● Towards the inverter

By sending the current to first Winding 1, then Winding 2, and finally Winding 3, the rotor turns forward. If it sends the current in the opposite order (3, 2, 1), it turns backward. On braking, the rotor's magnetic field generates a current in the windings that will recharge the battery.

In an induction motor, the rotor consists of an iron core surrounded by a series of connected copper bars. The presence of the stator's magnetic field induces a current in the copper of the rotor (hence the name "induction motor").

Induction motor
(Tesla Roadster)

Permanent-magnet motor
(Mitsubishi i-Miev)

This electric current transforms the iron of the rotor in turn into an electromagnet that plays the same role as the magnets of the permanent-magnet motor.

How is this important? These two types of motor give approximately the same performance at start up and full power, but each has its advantages. So, a permanent-magnet motor is more compact and 20% lighter than an induction motor of the same power. In contrast, the induction motor is cheaper to make and has better yields at low power over a very broad rpm range. It also copes much better with occasional bursts of power, such as a racing start.

Given their characteristics, it is thus logical to find permanent-magnet motors in small city models such as the Volkswagen e-Golf or the Mitsubishi i-Miev. Very high bursts of power are forbidden in the case of permanent-magnet motors, for beyond a certain threshold the magnetic fields can demagnetize the rotor's magnets and result in a breakdown. The electronics module is thus programmed to avoid this type of problem.

The development of permanent-magnet motors is nevertheless threatened by the risk of a crisis in the availability of the metals that compose the magnets, such as neodyme, scandium, samarium, and other rare earths, which come almost exclusively from China.

Induction motors are ideal for road sedans such as the Nissan Leaf and Tesla Models S and X. The latter two models' amazing bursts of speed prove the induction motor's ability to handle bursts of power. However, for cost reasons, induction motors are also found in small, inexpensive vehicles and many hybrids.

The battery

The range of an electric car depends on the size and state of charge of its battery. Today, the cars' batteries are based solely on the lithium-ion electrochemical reaction invented in 1990. This type of battery has conquered all battery-operated electrical appliances in an amazingly short period of under thirty years. After debuting in telephones and laptop computers, they moved on to power screw drivers, drills, and other portable power

Comparison

The Tesla Model S's 270 kW (367 hp) motor weighs 70 lb (32 kg). The Ford Fusion Sport's 2,700 cc V6 IEcoboost Turbo engine weighs 440 lb (200 kg) without fluids, exhaust, and gearbox, for a comparable power rating of 242 kW (325 hp).

The electric motor requires no maintenance, whereas the ICE needs regular care: You have to change the spark plugs, oil, and various filters at regular intervals and keep your eye on parts subject to wear, such as belts, tension rollers, clutch, catalytic converter, etc. The lifespan of an electric motor is put at 600,000 miles, that of an ICE at 200,000 miles.

© Oleg Alexandrov

Propulsion units of similar power: On the left, an electric motor with a single moving part, the rotor. On the right, a V6 turbo engine with several hundred moving parts.

tools and are now moving into bigger and bigger machines: lawn mowers, cars, trucks and light utility vehicles, and buses. We are even starting to see them in the 40-ton semis for 2019.

Don't say "lithium battery." Rather, say "lithium-ion cell" and save the word "battery" for an assembly of several cells. A cell is a simple small thing that looks like an AA battery such as we use in flashlights. A cell has a rated voltage of 3.6 V when it is charged and comes mainly in two forms: a cylinder or a flat pack. In both cases, the material that stores the electricity is a three-layer stack: an anode, a separator, and a cathode. In a cylindrical cell the sheet is rolled up on itself. In a rectangular cell a series of sheets are folded on themselves and stacked up.

Operation. A lithium-ion cell has two operating modes, charge and discharge, and can effectuate a large number of successive charging and discharging cycles, typically more than 1,000. A cell is composed of two electrodes: the cathode (positive electrode) and anode (negative electrode). The cathode is made of an oxide of several metals – mainly lithium, but also cobalt, nickel, aluminum, and manganese. The anode is made of graphite, a relatively cheap form of carbon. Between the two is an insulating but porous separator that is bathed in a liquid, the electrolyte, that is a solution of lithium salts in a carbonated solvent.

In charging, the electric current is sent to the cell, *i.e.*, the charger displaces the electrons from the cathode to the anode through an outside circuit. Each time an electron leaves the cathode, a lithium atom is turned into a positively-charged ion. This ion then moves through the liquid electrolyte and

3.6 volts

A lithium-ion cell normally has a voltage of 3.6 V, but can rise to 4.1 or 4.2 V when fully charged and drop to 2.9 V when discharged. Exceeding these limits can destroy the cell irreversibly. A smart charger specific to this type of battery is thus required.

Note. The reference values (2.9 V-3.6 V-4.2 V) can vary plus or minus a few tenths of a volt depending on the chemical composition of the cell used.

separator towards the anode, where it recombines with an electron that the charger has just sent. The anode is loaded with more and more lithium atoms. When the anode is saturated, the cell is charged.

In discharging, the opposite happens: A stream of electrons leaves the anode via the outside electric circuit, crosses the motor, and returns to the cathode, where the electrons recombine with the positive lithium ions that have crossed back through the separator. The lithium is unloaded from the anode, which thus returns to its initial state, the same as before charging began, and a new cycle can start.

Anode and cathode: The negative electrode is called the anode and the positive electrode is called the cathode.

Safety. Lithium-ion cells contain recyclable metals and a liquid, the electrolyte, that will not cause fires or acid burns. However, like a simple battery, a cell stores electricity and a short-circuit between its terminals can cause it to heat up strongly and cause contact fires and burns.

Today's most common wireless electricity applications call for voltages greater than 3.6 V. That is why several cells are assembled to make a battery. So, a garden tool that operates at 36 V has a battery composed of ten elements.

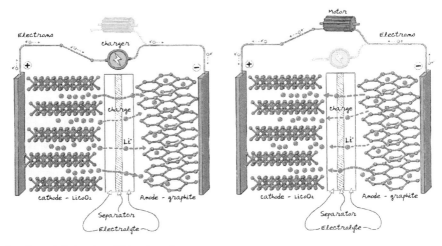

Charging and discharging a lithium-ion cell.

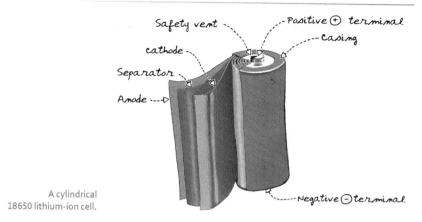

A cylindrical 18650 lithium-ion cell.

Electric cars operate at high voltage – usually on the order of 400 V – and to provide the capacity for the required range, the batteries sometimes weigh several hundred kilos. For reasons of mechanical behavior and handling ease, the cells are thus grouped in a small number of modules that can then be connected to each other to form a battery.

To improve its batteries' temperature regulation, Tesla, unlike the other EV makers, uses a very large number of small cells. For example, the Tesla Model S 85 has an imposing 85 kWh battery composed of 7,104 cylindrical cells. These cells are distributed among sixteen 21.6 V modules, so that the battery's rated voltage is 345 V when all the modules are connected in series. Each module contains 444 cylindrical cells of the 18650 format, *i.e.*, 18 mm in diameter and 65 mm

© Lead holder

On the left, two 6.5 cm-high cylindrical "18650" cells. On the right, the rectangular cells of one of the packs in a BMW i3.

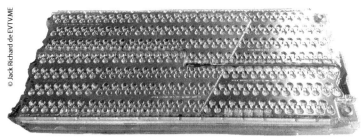

One of the sixteen modules in a Tesla Model S; it is an assembly of 444 identical "18650" cells.

in length. The cells in each module are assembled in groups of 74 cells connected in parallel and six of these groups are connected in series to form a module.

Tesla limits the charge in its cells to 4.2 V, so the battery's maximum end-of-charge voltage is 403 V.

Lithium. From the days of lead batteries we all remember above all how heavy lead is: One cubic decimeter of lead effectively weighs 11 kg (or the even more impressive 709 lb per cubic foot!). Today, lithium has become the most interesting metal for making batteries and its weight goes a long way in explaining this, for a cubic decimeter of lithium weights a mere 530 grams. If it did not oxidize so quickly, an ingot of lithium would float on water!

Lithium is the lightest metal on Earth. It is soft, silvery-grey, and blackens and oxidizes very quickly when it comes in contact with air or water. That is why it is not found in nature as a pure metal, but only in compounds, mainly salts such as lithium chloride. Lithium is abundant on Earth: The oceans contain 230 billion metric tons of lithium, or enough to make

Samples of metal lithium.

Salar de Uyuni in Bolivia.

automobile batteries for millions of years. However, our lithium does not come from seawater. It is extracted mainly from salt lakes, such as the Salar de Uyuni in Bolivia, the world's largest salt flat. The Salar de Uyuni contains half of the easily extractable lithium on the planet, enough for the batteries of more than 10 billion electric cars.

Despite its relative availability, lithium has become expensive, going from $5/kg in 2011 to $15/kg in 2018 following the increase in demand. The problem is not that of mining the metal. Rather, it is the lack of production and refining capacity. But it seems that 2019 is seeing a slight downturn in lithium price thanks to an increase in extraction capacities in Chile, China, and Australia.

A new avenue for producing lithium cheaply is being explored, that of "petrolithium." This lithium carbonate could be extracted from oil-well sludge. The extraction process should be quick and simple, but the quantities recoverable appear to be small.

The efforts made over the past five years are starting to increase the supply, but isn't demand rising even faster? To be continued...

Risks of failure. The risks of battery failure are limited. A battery contains no mechanical elements and generates little heat. Consequently, the manufacturers have no qualms about guaranteeing their performance for a long period. Tesla gives its batteries a lifetime warranty against all defects except the gradual reduction in charge with use, for which Tesla offers an 8-year warranty with unlimited mileage.

The failure that threatens lithium-ion cells is called metal plating. In certain unfavorable circumstances, under freezing conditions, with a reserve close to 0% and under a strong charging current, lithium ions adhere to the anode and cover it with a metal film. This undesirable layer stops the chemical reactions from taking place and reduces the battery's useful capacity, which could lead to total failure! Luckily, the onboard electronics takes care to limit the charging current under such conditions. Nevertheless, depleting the battery completely and then rushing to connect to a supercharger is strongly disadvised if the thermometer is down in the "freezer" range!

Fire or explosive risks. Fires caused by lithium batteries are extremely rare but spectacular. How are they triggered? One possible cause is lithium's great sensitivity to oxidation. As long as the cell remains airtight, you have nothing to worry about. But if it is punctured, the lithium will come in contact with the airborne humidity, oxidize, and thus get hot. This heating can in turn cause the electrolyte to evaporate and the cell to explode due to a sudden pressure increase.

Another possible cause is overcharging. In a greatly over-charged cell, the temperature rises, lithium ions build up on the anode and reduce its useful surface area, which causes the ions to build up even faster on the remaining exposed areas of the anode, and on it goes. This "thermal divergence" reaction, as it is called, can also cause the electrolyte to evaporate, with the same harmful consequences as those of accidental oxidation. Oxygen may be given off, which will worsen the situation by making it more difficult to put out the fire.

Luckily, the chemical compositions of electric vehicle batteries and the electronics that oversees temperature and charge levels protect against these risks. The known cases of fires or explosions of lithium-ion cells have occurred almost solely in portable devices (phones and power tools) and in situations with a combination of unfavorable factors: a poorly cooled housing, overcharging due to the use of an inappropriate charger, even a design flaw in the device. A few cases of fires in electric cars have been reported, but their number remains low. The U.S. Department of Transportation has published statistics on this subject according to which electric cars are one-fifth as likely as an ICE car to have a fire per driving mile.

The following instructions must be heeded for lithium batteries, as for all batteries, moreover: Do not puncture, deform, overcharge, or overheat.

Weight. Having a large range is the most desirable feature of an electric car. This is achieved at the expense of the price and weight of the lithium battery, which remains the heaviest element in an electric car. Up until 2015, a small electric city car with a range of scarcely 60 miles (100 km) was standard. However, the constant advances made in battery designs now make it possible to offer 2019 models with typical ranges of 160 mi to 250 mi or even more under real road conditions without increasing their price.

Price. The question that all future electric car buyers are asking today is when the electric versions will be sold at the same prices as their ICE counterparts. The battery continues to be a problem in 2019 models, even though battery prices have dropped 15% over the past ten years. The cost of the battery accounts for slightly less than half of the car's price. This cost is due mainly to the kilos of materials of which it is made, for, due to automated manufacturing, labor costs add mere pennies to the overall bill. The constant reduction in the weight required to store a kilowatt-hour of energy will thus remain the key factor in electric car price developments.

Performances. Many more improvements are expected and will continue to reduce battery size and price. The huge efforts being made in the area of lithium chemistry lead us

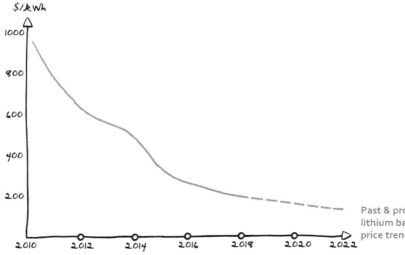

Past & projected lithium battery price trend.

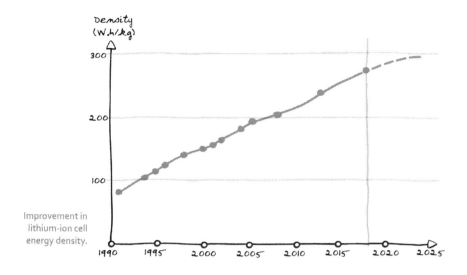

Improvement in
lithium-ion cell
energy density.

to believe that the technology's theoretical limit of about 300 watt-hours/kg will be reached by 2021-2022, whereas today we are still at only 150 Wh/kg (2019 models).

However, the improvements will not stop in a few years, once the current lithium-ion technology limit is reached. The wealth of research currently under way gives us glimpses of substantial additional gains in the future with silicon anodes and other tricks that could increase battery performance by a factor of five. For example, Stordot, Enevate, Seeo, and Maxwell Technologies, acquired by Tesla in January 2019, are some of the new kids on the block that are developing promising new battery-improving techniques. These companies are promising energy densities of close to 500 Wh/kg in under three years. But will they succeed?

Still, the ransom of success is also the possibility of the inverse effect. Demand for the basic raw materials is increasing by about 20% a year. The law of supply and demand will result in skyrocketing prices for lithium, cobalt, and manganese, which are the batteries' key elements. To what extent is this likely to slow down the price drop? That is obviously hard to predict.

Energy and yield

Weight of the energy reserve: 80 to 1 in gasoline's favor.

A Tesla S battery stores 72 Wh/lb. Its rival, the BMW 335, burns gasoline, which contains 5,900 Wh/lb !

Energy yield: 6 to 1 in electricity's favor.

The Tesla covers 1 mile on 3.6 lb of battery. It thus uses 260 Wh/mi. The BMW, with its rated mileage of 23 mpg, uses 1,600 Wh of energy per mile, or six times more than the Tesla.

Energy price: 3 to 1 in electricity's favor.

With regular gas selling at $2.50/gal and consumption of 23 mpg, the BMW's driver spends $10.90 on the energy needed to drive 100 mi. With electricity selling at $0.12/kWh and 26 kWh used to cover 100 mi, the Tesla uses $3.12'worth of energy.

Recycling. At the ends of their lives (75% of initial capacity), most electric car batteries can be reused to store stationary energy. This is a logical complement to the PV panels-electric car tandem. Currently, about one-third of EOL (end-of-life) batteries are given a new lease on life in energy storage cabinets, usually in companies, but also in private homes. The prices of the home batteries sold by automakers should drop sharply in the future with the rise in their reuse. Tesla (PowerWall), Mercedes, BMW, and Nissan (xStorage) are already active on this front.

What about discardable batteries? They can be recycled, even though this is not yet a frequent practice. EOL batteries ready to be recycled just started coming on the market in 2018 and their numbers are still small. Yet recycling lithium batteries does not pose major problems, for they contain only very small amounts of volatile or corrosive materials harmful to human health: The liquid electrolytes are not acid and give off polluting gases only in the case of a fire, not when they are handled cold.

In contrast, separating the various metals in the cathodes and housings calls for facilities and chemical expertise that are not at everyone's disposal, and discarding them in the surroundings creates ecological risks. Recycling them is required by law in Europe and many countries elsewhere, with the cost borne by the original equipment manufacturer (OEM). Since recycling the lithium, cobalt, and other metals in these batteries does not seem to be a profitable activity in its own right, the recyclers will have to be cofinanced by the battery manufacturers or automakers.

Several companies have already set up their own recycling schemes. The best known is probably that of the originally German company Kuehne + Nagel (now based in Switzerland), which proposes to take charge of the lithium battery's entire life-cycle logistics, from the factory that provides the components to the battery plant and on to the car assembly lines. After that, for the recycling per se, Kuehne + Nagel will recover the spent batteries from the car dealers or battery manufacturers and ship them to recycling facilities, which will in turn supply the materials for making new batteries.

Recycling facilities are starting to crop up slowly all over Europe. One example is Umicore Battery Recycling in Belgium. In Canada, Li-Cycle has developed a recycling chain that can recycle 100% of the battery materials. The company is working on a pilot plant to recycle batteries and plans to start with a processing capacity of 5,000 metric tons of batteries a year.

In the United States, Redwood Materials – a company created recently in Redwood, California (20 miles from Tesla's Fremont plant) – seems to be extremely interested in recycling lithium-ion batteries. While it is keeping an extremely low profile, the company's only known managers are J.B. Straubel, Chief Technical Officer at Tesla, and Andrew Stevenson, who left his position of Special Projects Manager at Tesla in June 2018. Might this be indicative of a future Tesla battery recycling facility in the works?

Not all lithium is the same...

Several types of lithium-ion cell are found on the market, each with its advantages and drawbacks. These variations are referred to by abbreviations that highlight the proportions of the various metals making up the metal cathode. The two main families of batteries are called "NCM or NMC" and "NCA," but "LFP" and other families also exist. When the abbreviation for the metals is followed by a number, this indicates the proportions of the metals used. So, an NCM811 battery contains 8 parts nickel for 1 part cobalt and 1 part manganese.

NCM (Lithium Nickel Cobalt Manganese)

NCM batteries combine all the main characteristics required of car batteries: capacity, safety, and ability to generate high voltages if necessary. They generate little heat and thus are the best choice for large vehicles and those that lack controlled cooling. One-third of today's electric cars use NCM batteries.

NCM chemistry is advancing by leaps and bounds. Each new version improves battery capacity or life and reduces its cost price. For example, LG Chem began manufacturing NCM811 cathodes in 2018 to replace the preceding generation of NCM523 and NCM424 cathodes. The new cells have similar capacities, but are more compact and – something very important – contain half as much cobalt and thus cost a lot less to make. We expect them in the Nissan Leaf 2019 and in BMW i5 in 2021.

The South Korean company SK Innovation is taking another path, for its large rectangular cells use a gelled electrolyte and a silicon-graphite anode. Its cells are found in the Kia Soul EV and several Mercedes Benz hybrids, among others.

NCA (Lithium Nickel Cobalt Aluminum)

NCA batteries have excellent capacity and lifespans, greater than those of NCM batteries. Long considered to be rather expensive, they now (in 2019 models) offer the best ratio of price to capacity, but are rather tricky to manage: Precise planning of charging and discharging is necessary to avoid possible deterioration. One-third of today's electric cars, almost exclusively Teslas, use NCA batteries.

N **Nickel.** Nickel is a fairly abundant metal. It is shiny, harder and heavier than iron (relative density of 8, *i.e.* 8 kg/l), with a cost price of about $11/kg.

C **Cobalt.** Cobalt is very close to nickel. It is not very abundant and is used in dyes ("cobalt blue") and batteries. Cobalt is often extracted from copper ore. Half of the world's cobalt is found in Democratic Republic of Congo, where unethical mining practices and political strife are rampant. The price of cobalt was more than $90/kg in spring 2018, but is falling sharply thanks to its decreasing percentage in modern batteries and an increase in production capacity. About half of the cobalt used is then recycled, but its relative scarcity and price are leading to its' being replaced by other, more common, metals.

M **Manganese.** A silvery-white metal that is slightly lighter than iron. It is found above all as an oxide in iron ore and is used to harden steel. It is abundant and cheap. Its cost price is $2.30/kg.

F **Iron.** A well-known greyish-white metal with a relative density of 7.8. Iron makes up one-third of Earth's core! Iron is used everywhere, including to make chassis. Procuring it is not a problem. It costs about $0.10/kg on world markets.

P **Phosphorus.** Phosphorus is a non metal known for its phosphorescence. It has a relative density of a little less than 2. It can be extracted from urine and guano, but the industrial method uses phosphoric rock that is heated in ovens. This rock comes from Morocco, China, and South Africa. Agriculture uses almost all of the output in the form of phosphates (phosphorus oxides). The world's reserves are limited, with the known reserves to last some 100 or so years at the current rate of use. The phosphate from which phosphorus is extracted currently sells for about $0.50/kg.

LFP (Lithium Iron Phosphate)

LFP batteries are very reliable but bulky, because they have a voltage of 3.2 V instead of 3.6 V for the other types. They have good lifespans and tolerate overcharging and strong currents well. On the negative side of the balance sheet, they tend to lose their charge rather quickly, even when they are not in use. This can lead to useless high electricity consumption in the case of cars that are driven little but remain connected to their chargers. LFP batteries thus are better suited for use in heavily-used vehicles, such as buses. On the other hand, they offer the advantage of not depending on cobalt supplies. Sixteen percent of electric cars currently use them.

Other more esoteric chemistries complete the range of lithium-ion cell types, but do not have the same advantages of cost, compactness, or lifespan.

As the following table shows, lithium-ion cell manufacturing is in the hands of only five suppliers, namely, in order of importance, Panasonic (Japan), BYD (China), LG Chem (South Korea), Nissan-AESC (Japan), and Samsung SDI (South Korea).

That mysterious BMS

If you were ever seized one day by the desire to decipher the technical description of an electric vehicle, you must

Maker (n alphabetical order)	Model	Type	Supplier of the cells	Shape
BMW	I3	NCM	Samsung SDI	rectangle
BYD (Chine)	E6	LFP	BYD	rectangle
BYD-Daimler (Chine)	Denza 400	LFP	BYD	rectangle
Chevrolet	Bolt	NCM	LG Chem	rectangle
Citroën	e-Mehari	LFP	Bolloré	rectangle
Fiat/Chrysler	500ᵉ	NCM	Samsung SDI	rectangle
Ford	Focus	NCM	LG Chem	rectangle
Hyundai	Ioniq EV	NCM	LG Chem	rectangle
Hyundai	Kona EV	NCM	LG Chem	rectangle
Kia	Soul EV	NCM-gel	Sk Innovation	rectangle
Nissan	Leaf 2016	NCA	AESC – GSR Capital	rectangle
Nissan	Leaf 2018	NCM	LG Chem	rectangle
Nissan	Leaf E-Plus	NCM	LG Chem	rectangle
Opel/Vauxhall	Ampera-E	NCM	LG Chem	rectangle
Renault	Zoé	NCM	LG Chem	rectangle
Smart		NCM	LiTech	cylinder
Tesla	3	NCA	Panasonic	cylinder
Tesla	S	NCA	Panasonic	cylinder
Tesla	X	NCA	Panasonic	cylinder
Volkswagen	e-Golf	NCM	Samsung SDI	rectangle
Volkswagen	e-up!	NCM	Samsung SDI	rectangle
Volkswagen	I.D. 2019	NCM	LG Chem	rectangle

have seen the "BMS." This electronic box is the Battery Management System, designed to keep the battery in good working order. Why is it so important?

The batteries are composed of a large number of cells. Even though manufacturers are careful to choose all identical cells, tiny differences among them always subsist. Some cells will thus discharge faster than others or store a little more energy than their neighbors and thus discharge a tiny bit slower.

Imbalancing? The big problem with lithium batteries is that these tiny differences increase, little by little, with the charging/discharging cycles. The cells are said to be imbalanced. This imbalance carries the risk of overloading certain cells and discharging other cells completely, two situations that can destroy the battery!

The BMS is connected to an impressive mass of electric wires linking it to each of the terminals of each cell in the battery. For example, a Tesla S P90 battery contains 7,104 cells. Thanks to all these connections, the BMS checks the voltage on each cell and stops battery charging or discharging as soon as a single cell reaches its maximum or minimum voltage. So, the BMS is what decides when the charge screen displays "0%" or "100%." It takes advantage of these actions to memorize the battery's degree of imbalance.

A small BMS circuit that controls 12 lithium-ion cells.

Rebalancing! The role of the BMS is much more than simply checking voltage levels. At the end of charging – typically between 95% and 100% – the BMS discharges the most charged cells and tops up the charges in the most weakly charged cells until the cells are balanced again. Since the differences to smooth out are tiny, the currents are weak, so the connections can be made with very fine copper wires. The BMS's low-profile but constant action is the true secret of the electric car battery's long life. Without the BMS, the lithium batteries would live one-tenth as long while losing capacity at each charging/discharging cycle.

Temperature

Lithium batteries cannot be charged risk-free below 0 °C (32 °F). At freezing temperatures, the anode starts to clump the metallic lithium, which reduces the cells' capacities. To avoid this phenomenon, the electronic charge controllers preheat the battery before beginning charging or limit the charging speed. This can become a real problem for cars parked outdoors in winter in Scandinavia, Russia, or Quebec! Inversely, if the temperatures are very high, battery life can be affected by recharging too quickly or storing the battery too long with 100% recharging.

Since all the charging operations heat the batteries, the controllers constantly check the temperature and trigger battery cooling or reduce the charging current, if need be.

Luckily for drivers, the acceptable temperature range for discharging is much broader than for recharging. Consequently, there is nothing to prevent driving in all types of weather.

Preserving battery life

Preserving battery life is a complicated art, for you have to avoid voltages that are too low, sudden recharging in cold weather, and high charging currents if the battery is almost fully charged. All of this must be managed, on pain of damaging seriously or even destroying the battery! No driver can constantly manage all these parameters. So, it is the car's computer's job to check the battery charging levels, charging times, and temperature to avoid stressing the battery.

This supervision is usually invisible to the user, but is sometimes noticed and can create some surprises. For example, when a fast charger usually takes 10 minutes to recharge a battery from 60 to 80%, you prepare to start up ten minutes later with an almost fully-charged battery. However, in some cases you may see that the charge level has risen only a couple of percent. That may be because the temperature rose and forced the computer to reduce the charging power. That can be frustrating, even though you know that it was done for the "good" of the battery!

There's one thing that the computer cannot do: foresee the driver's intentions. That is where careful charge-level management can preserve battery life. Choosing the maximum charge level is the best example of this. For routine trips, it is better to charge no more than 80-90%. Only when a long trip is planned should you let the charger go to 100%. Indeed, even though it is true particularly for soaring summer temperatures, leaving a battery at high voltage levels for a long time reduces its life.

And in the case of a long period of idleness, it is recommended to leave the battery at a low or moderate charge level. For example, if you leave a 60%-charged battery in the garage for a month, you will recover it with a 30-40% charge without lessening its lifespan.

Avoiding draining batteries to the 0% mark is also beneficial. The usual recommendation is to use the last five percent only when absolutely necessary and to plan routine trips so as not to have to drop that low in order to reduce the risks of damaging the electrodes irreversibly.

The "brick" risk

Discharging a lithium battery completely never happens! Well, actually, it should never happen, because that is not at all good for battery life! It will happen only if you leave an electric car displaying 0% charge for several weeks. During this time, the battery will continue to drain below the 0% mark of its authorized range, meaning that the cells' voltages will gradually fall below 2 V and even lower. Resuscitating a battery that has been damaged by being totally drained may be impossible. In that case, the battery is said to have been turned into a brick!

That is why the manufacturers stipulate in their sales contracts – in very fine print, of course – that a drained battery should never be left for more than a few days before being recharged. The experience garnered by battery manufacturers nevertheless improves things from year to year. So, the Tesla Model S can withstand remaining at the fatal "0% mark" for at least a month thanks to a deep sleep mode that minimizes the battery's self-consumption.

Why does the battery deteriorate so little?

The manufacturers want to provide their customers with batteries that can be used from 0 to 100% in all circumstances and throughout the life of the car. They thus all implement a strategy of masking a guaranteed capacity within a slightly

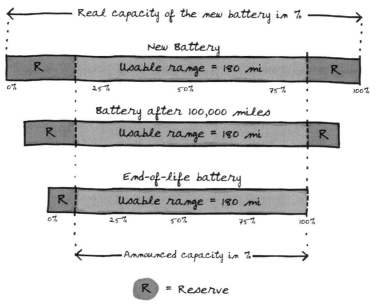

Strategy to preserve battery life by masking the real range.
The safety margin ("reserve") accounts for 10-30% of the new battery's real autonomy.

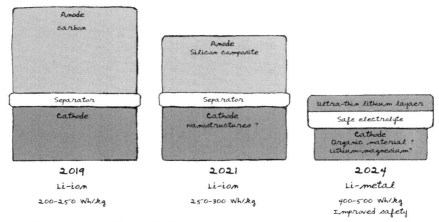

Expected advances in lithium-ion batteries.

higher real capacity. So, the customer does not see the car's real range drop while the battery loses capacity. Only when the "safety cushion" is used up do the range numbers start to fall.

This method must not be seen as misleading consumers, but rather as a way to simplify the user's life by applying, unknown to them, the best possible strategies for preserving battery autonomy.

Careful! Just because the manufacturer has done its utmost to avoid premature aging of the battery does not mean that you may ignore the rules of good practice.

The future of batteries

Improved battery performance is what will make – or break – the success of the electric car over the next ten years. The most prestigious laboratories in the world, battery manufacturers, and manufacturing startups are working on this: LG, Panasonic, Samsung, MIT, Stanford, Nexeon, Saft, and many, many more are spending millions of dollars to improve battery performance. Researchers are testing the electrodes and electrolytes of the future and are already pushing back today's limits. The new developments in laboratory testing today will be in our cars in five years' time and the discoveries made in 2019 could go into production over the next ten years.

The transmission

The electric motor offers sufficient power over a very large range of operating regimes, typically from 0 to more than 10,000 rpm. It can even provide its maximum torque on starting, which eliminates the need for a gearbox. The transmission in an electric car is thus very simple and compact: There is only one gear train – usually two pairs – designed to reduce the motor's speed of rotation, which can rise to 10,000 rpm, in order to entrain the wheels, which turn at only a few hundred rpm.

Example: An electric car motor turns at 10,000 rpm at a speed of 80 mph and has a gear step-down factor of 10. At that speed, the motor is thus turning at 166 revolutions per second whereas the wheel, which has a circumference of 7 feet, is doing only 16.6 revolutions per second.

© Cschirp

Motor-transmission group of the Volkswagen e-Golf.
In the background: Permanent-magnet motor.
On the left: Step-down gears.
In the foreground: Differential and two gimbals that entrain the wheels.

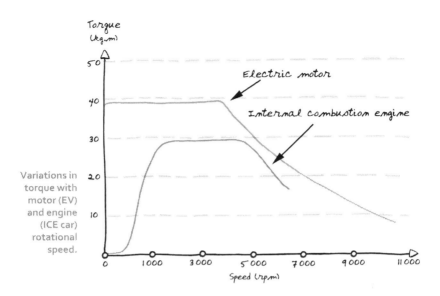

Torque (kg-m)

Electric motor

Internal combustion engine

Variations in torque with motor (EV) and engine (ICE car) rotational speed.

Speed (rpm)

An electric motor delivers maximum torque – rotational force – as soon as it starts up. Next, if you continue to floor the accelerator, this torque remains constant until the motor reaches its maximum power. As soon as the motor gives its full power, the torque declines and the car accelerates less and less strongly until it reaches its top speed. The very flat shape of the torque-over-rpm plot is the mathematical expression of the great driving smoothness of an electric car.

Let's compare the above plot with that produced by a vehicle with an ICE of similar power. The tricky period during which the gas-powered car's clutch has to deal with the first turns of the wheel is clearly visible, as are the hiccups in the torque plot with each change of speed.

Speed selector and start/stop button in the BMW i3.
D = drive,
N = neutral,
R = reverse,
P = parking brake by blocking the transmission.

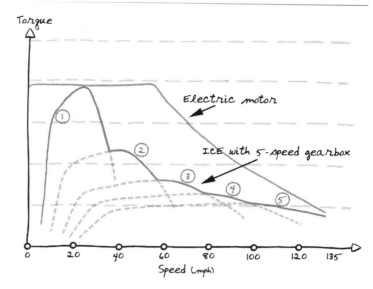

Changes in torque with changing speed for an electric car and five-speed gas-powered car.

The driving force exiting the step-down gears is sent to a conventional differential that distributes the effort between the two wheels of the drive axle. Its indispensable presence enables the two wheels to turn at slightly different speeds when necessary, for example, in tight curves.

We also notice that no gears are needed to reverse. To back up, reversing the direction in which the motor turns suffices. Such a feature could also be frightening at times, for no one wants to reverse at 60 mph. That is why the speed when reversing is limited electronically by the car's computer.

One last reassuring detail: As in automatic gearboxes, the transmission also includes a lock that blocks the wheels when the lever is in the parking position "P."

The electronics module

The last element in an electric car is the electronic control box. It is rather voluminous, for it contains several important components, including the car's computer, intelligent controllers such as the ABS and traction control, but also and above all two power-controlling elements, namely, the

The electronics module of the Volkswagen e-up! We see six orange cables at the top of the module. They are, from left to right, the three connections to the three-phase motor, hookup to the charging socket, and two cables that go to the battery.

charger and the inverter that controls the motor. This last element handles large power fluxes of 100 kW and more.

The motors, be they induction or permanent-magnet motors, must be supplied with alternating current. And since the battery delivers direct current only, a conversion unit has to be inserted between the two. This conversion device, which is called an inverter, does not have a perfect 100% yield. The two or three percent that is lost in the conversion of dozens of kilowatt-hours of power takes the form of heat loss comparable to that of a clothes iron. The electronics box must thus be cooled, sometimes by air flows, but usually by the liquid coolant that also regulates the battery temperature. It is often placed very close to the motor to minimize the lengths of the power cables required.

The onboard computer gets various inputs: the battery's state of health (voltage, temperature, charge level), vehicle status (speed, acceleration, braking, curve angle, etc.), and the driver's intentions (ignition key, brake and accelerator pedals, and various switches and controls). It determines from all these data how much power must be sent to the motor under normal driving conditions or to the battery in the case of slowing down. It also takes on all the functions that one is entitled to expect from a modern car, such as central locking, directional control, releasing the brakes, and many other functions that depend on the car's level of sophistication.

The inverter can deliver three synchronized alternating electric currents with variable frequencies and voltages to provide the motor with the power and speed requested by the accelerator. At other times, during the braking recovery phases, for example, the motor works like an alternator and generates an alternating current that the inverter must rectify to produce direct current to recharge the battery.

The core component of the inverter is a set of six power switches, each of which connects one of the two terminals of the battery to one of the three terminals of the three-phase motor. They are mounted directly on the connectors of the thick orange cables that link the electronic module to the battery and motor. This makes it possible to power a single winding of the motor at a time in one or the other direction.

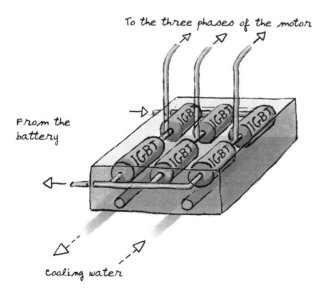

To the three phases of the motor

From the battery

cooling water

Diagram of an electric vehicle's power inverter. At any given moment, a single IGBT switch in the upper row and a single IGBT switch in the lower row are closed. This makes it possible to power a single winding of the motor at a time in one or the other direction.

The six power switches are very sturdy electronic components called IGBTs (insulated gate bipolar transistors) that can switch from the "conducting" state to the open (non-conducting) state up to 20,000 times a second, which enables the computer to regulate the used or recovered power level with great precision and makes the car so smooth and pleasant to drive. Since they carry strong currents in the hundreds of amperes, they are mounted in an aluminum housing crisscrossed by a liquid coolant that carries off the inevitable calories that are generated.

The onboard charger is similar to a conventional battery charger: It transforms the 110 V or 220 V current from the grid into direct current and sends it to the battery. Like the rest of the car's functions, charging is controlled by the onboard computer, which makes certain that the charge level, intensity, and temperature limits are not exceeded and battery life is not imperiled. In some cases, the charger is located in a separate box, usually close to the charging socket, rather than in the main electronics module. In the Tesla Model 3, however, it is incorporated directly in the battery located in the floor of the car.

The charging connection

The simplest way to recharge an electric car is to plug a simple charger, which is almost always provided with the car, into a household outlet. In North America, the home outlet is standardized and delivers 120 volts. Intensity is usually limited by a 15 A breaker. This solution has the advantage of not requiring any modifications in the fixed wiring, with tens of millions of such outlets available around the country. However, it does have drawbacks: Charging is extremely slow (typically 1.5 kilowatts) and the connection is not always very reliable. The plugs and outlets are grounded, of course, but current runs through the conductors in the cable at all times. Handling the cable when it is raining or snowing is thus far from risk-free.

© BMI

Recharging from a home outlet with the manufacturer-supplied charging cable

That is why most electric car owners install a wall box with a permanently connected cable to which a special "electric car" outlet is mounted. Wall boxes are also called EVSE, the acronym for Electric Vehicle Supply Equipment. Automakers sell these "Level 2" charging stations with their cars as options, but excellent ones can be found on the market at cheaper prices, *i.e.*, from about $500 to $900. They can deliver 3-22 kilowatts from a single- or three-phase home electricity supply and are safe: The cable carries current only when it is connected to the vehicle and the insulation is checked by the car's electronics.

The home charging stations may be placed outside and are weather-proof. They contain their own circuit breaker to protect the circuit from overloads and short circuits, a contact breaker activated by a command from the vehicle to start or stop charging, and status lights: energized, connected, charging, or error. Optional accessories include a meter and even a badge reader for paying one's consumption.

In North America, charging from a home outlet is extremely slow, therefore installing a 220 V line to power a wall box is highly recommended. To facilitate this operation, the purchase of a wall box or upgrading the electricity line is often subsidized. Also check with your local utility company to see if there are electricity rebates to take advantage of in your area. In many areas businesses, multi-family apartment buildings, and public agencies are offered rebates of up to $5,000 or even more by utility companies.

Tax credits or incentives from $500 to $1,500 exists in 60% of U.S. states for residents who install a home charger. In Canada, Quebec subsidizes a wallbox to the tune of CAN$600 for an average purchase.

Specific sockets

Specific charging sockets that combine power, safety, and sturdiness have been designed for electric cars. They combine a conventional electrical outlet, an energizing power switch, and a connection between the vehicle and charger. For fast chargers, additional prongs are provided to transmit the necessary high-voltage current. Everything would actually have been very simple if the Japanese, Europeans, and Americans had not decided to use systems that were incompatible with each other.

Each time a new development hits the market, it takes years to adopt a common standard in order to make users' lives

An EVChargeKing wall box supplied with monophase 220V current that delivers 3 or 7 kW.

easier. After more than a century, all the countries in the world still do not agree on which side of the road to drive! What, then, can we say about the home electrical outlets for which huge differences exist between Europe, the United Kingdom, and the United States? At least for the western countries, the standards headache is limited to four types of connection that are listed in a single internationally-recognized standard bearing the simple name of IEC 62196-3. One of them, Type 1, is one of the most widely used in the U.S. and Canada.

Safety. When you plug your car into the charging socket, the system must first detect whether the plugs are connected correctly on the vehicle and wall box sides, the plugs are locked into place, and the system is grounded correctly. Contact is made only if all these conditions are met.

Type 1

The Type 1 socket originated in Japan (it is also called a Yazaki socket) but is also used in North America. It can take 110 or 230 V and is limited to 16 amps, for a power of 7.4 kW for a 230 V line. It does not support three-phase con- nection and is not used in Europe.

Monophase Type 1 charging socket, 7 kW maximum.

Type 2 and "CCS Combo" connectors

The Type 2 connector is by far the most widely used outside North America. It is sometimes called the "Mennekes socket" after the German company that developed it. It allows connection to the grids in single-phase 230 V or three-phase 400 V mode – the voltages accessible in private homes. The allowed

The Type 2 charging socket is more and more popular. It is also now the European standard.

The CCS charging socket is a variation on the Type 2 that is used for DC fast charging, for example, on BMWs and Volkswagens.

power goes from 3.7 kW in single-phase charging to 43.5 kW in three-phase charging. The European Community has designated the Type 2 socket a standard in Europe.

The Type 2 socket is usually one with a non-removable cable connected to the charging station. It is plugged into the vehicle's socket directly. After use it is hung up on a bracket, just like a gas pump hose. Many electric cars are delivered with a male/female Type 1 or Type 2 cable to connect to charging stations with flush-mounted sockets.

The variant of the Type 2 socket with two additional prongs is also the most widely used for DC fast charging. In that case, it is called a "Combo" or "CCS" for Combined Charging System. The CCS cable is always one with the wall box and the socket is connected to the vehicle directly.

"ChaDeMo" socket

"ChaDeMo" fast-charging sockets deliver up to 62.5 kW DC. They are used by all Japanese electric cars, but are also found on Kias and Hyundais.

A lot of ChaDeMo fast chargers are found in North America and, of course, in Japan. They offer the particularity of incorporating intelligent dialog wiring between the car and charging station so that the charging station will not deliver

A ChaDeMo charging socket.

power if the connectors are not secure. Thanks to this smart connection, the charger constantly checks the charge intensity and duration that it must supply without running the risk of damaging the battery.

On the lighter side, in Japanese, *O cha demo ikaga desuka* translates as "Let's have a cup of tea while it is charging."

Tesla

The Tesla connector is present on all Tesla destination chargers and superchargers. Supercharger connectors supply electrical power to Tesla vehicles at up to 120 kW *via* a direct current (DC) connection. The cable is always attached to the charging station; the cable ends with a male connector that plugs directly in the vehicle's charge port.

On the left, a type 2 connector. On the right, the Tesla connector used in North America.

What if you don't have the right socket?

Despite the increasing spread of Type 2 sockets, EV drivers are regularly confronted with problems of incompatibility between their vehicles and charging stations designed for

105

another system. A car is never delivered with all possible adapters. Luckily, adapters such as a "Type 1 to Type 2 station" cables or a Type 2 male-female extension are easy to find from the makers or on online accessory sales sites. And in the worst case, the charger provided by the OEM will always let you initiate slow charging on any conventional household electricity socket, of which there are millions.

Tesla
and the others

Tesla, the only exclusively electric automaker

Tesla, a company founded in 2003 and unknown to the public at large even ten years ago, has now become synonymous with the electric car. Its first vehicle, the Tesla Roadster, was launched in 2008. The Roadster was followed by the large Model S sedan and Model X SUV, and their success quickly boosted Tesla's stock market value. Since late 2017 Tesla has also been delivering the very succesful Model 3, a mid-range sedan that is competing directly with the BMW Series 3 and Audi A4, never mind the announcement of an electric tractor-trailer and a new generation Roadster in the years to come!

Tesla is now ranked among the top five listed automakers in the world, behind Toyota, Daimler, and Volkswagen and neck-and-neck with BMW and General Motors. Yet Tesla has sold fewer than 532,000 cars in ten years, whereas General Motors delivers 10 million cars each year. However, while the legacy automakers' production figures are more or less stable year-on-year, Tesla's growth has been impressive;

Tesla Model S

It sold more cars in 2018 than it sold in all the years since its founding. What is the source of this impressive enthusiasm on the part of the public and investors?

The Model S sedan and Model X SUV are ranked among the best on the market. The Model S has been named the best of all cars ever sold, electric and ICE combined, by a host of car journalists, users' associations, and other critics. However, the Tesla Motors adventure, more than the quality of its products, is what is revolutionizing the car industry with its approach.

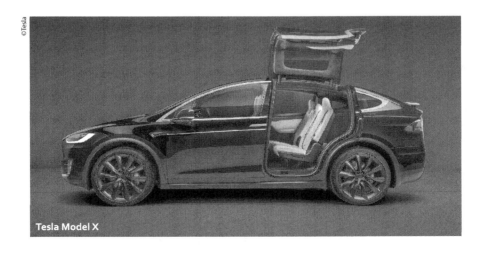

Tesla Model X

A different approach

There are many reasons for Tesla's dominance of the electric vehicle market, but these reasons themselves are justified by a corporate strategy aimed 100% at the renewable energy market. Tesla's goal is not just to sell cars, but to provide global solutions that will make it possible to free human-kind from fossil fuels. That is why Tesla also sells solar collectors and home batteries and has invested so heavily in a supercharger network placed judiciously along the major travel routes in the U.S., Canada, and Europe. Above all, the multinational is organized completely differently from conventional major automakers.

Byron Carrier of Earthly Religion has immortalized Tesla's mission: "To accelerate the world's transition to sustainable energy."

A vision of the future worthy of science fiction

We can get a glimpse of the next stages with the coming appearance of other products that should revolutionize all road transportation segments, *i.e.*, the "Model Y" unveiled in March 2019, the "Tesla Semi" truck, whose prototypes were already on the road in early 2019, the sporty "Roadster 2" in 2020, and so on. Even when you know that Tesla often delivers its new products with a certain delay, the prices and performances of these future vehicles are already causing all its rivals to break out in a cold sweat!

Tesla Model 3

However, Tesla's ambitions go beyond simply selling cars. With its activities in photovoltaic collectors and energy storage in stationary batteries connected to the grid, the company is setting up an entire sustainable energy ecosystem. As it puts all its money on the electrification of transportation, Tesla is convinced that the future belongs to driverless cars. That is why all Tesla cars are already equipped with sensors that will enable them to drive themselves one day! If you want to own

Tesla's "S3XY" strategy

Tesla's big boss, Elon Musk, said it as of the company's founding: "Our goal is to accelerate the advent of sustainable transport by bringing compelling mass market electric cars to market as soon as possible."

Since it is out of the question for a corporate debutant to attack a mass market directly, Tesla began in 2003 by selling a high-performance sporty roadster in small numbers: about 100 a year.

The experience that it acquired enabled it, in a second phase, to attack the larger luxury sedan market with the Models S and X, which sell at the rate of some 100,000 cars a year.

The third stage was the 2017 launch of a finally more affordable model, the Model 3, the annual sales of which reached 138,000 cars in 2018. With the Model 3 now the U.S.' best-selling luxury vehicle, the next step will be the introduction of the Model Y. This seven-seat crossover (a third row is added in the back) is expected to start rolling out of the Spark, Nevada, gigafactory en masse in 2020.

Tesla's marketing department intends to use the models' designations "S3XY" (sexy) to full advantage.

The Model Y SUV unveiled in March 2019 is derived from the Model 3 and should be available in volume in 2020.

©Tesla

a self-driving car, all you have to do is order a Tesla with the "full self-driving capability" option. This futuristic option is in the catalog, but Tesla specifies that it does not yet know when the option will be fully operational and its availability date will depend on software validation and local regulatory approval.

Tesla also intends to activate – at an as-yet-unspecified date – its "Tesla Network," that is, a fleet of driverless autonomous taxis to which the owners of self-driving Teslas will be able to contribute, and be paid for that to boot! Imagine, for a second, that, as you sleep, your car can leave the garage and spend the night earning its living as a taxi. Surprising, don't you think?

No dealers...

The day-to-day life of an automaker such as Tesla is very different from that of other car makers: Neither sales nor customer service resemble usual practices. Tesla's sales and maintenance structure is closer to Apple's than to Volkswagen's.

The software on board Teslas is updated frequently, wirelessly, and without the owner's intervention. No need to call the vehicles into a dealer's for a "quick update," which is always stressful. On the contrary, Tesla owners regularly discover that improvements have been added to the car. One example is the Easy Entry function, added at the end of 2017, that raises the steering wheel and retracts the seat temporarily so you can slide into your Model S more easily. And as recently as in March 2019, all Model 3 performances were updated "over the air", with a top speed increased by 7 mph and a range increased from 310 miles to 325 miles.

An electric car is much simpler and more reliable than an ICE car and often spends much less time being serviced. That does away with the need for a myriad of dealers and agents to maintain a whole fleet of vehicles and, without an enormous dealers' network, direct sales over the Internet become an obvious choice. There is no future for car salespeople at Tesla: Customers must simply log onto Tesla's website to order a new car.

...buying online instead

Tesla manages all its customer service online. Your mobile phone may be used to request a test ride, order a car, schedule a maintenance appointment, and manage your car battery and heating remotely. Even opening and closing your car's doors is done through your phone. Customers no longer need to go to a physical store. This is so true that Tesla closed in 2019 many brick-and-mortar shops that opened in the past years, with just a few being kept as showcases. If you stop by these showrooms, you will receive explanations and test rides, but don't expect the staff to sell the cars or bargain over discounts. Consequently, the American consumers' association Consumer Reports once again put the make at the top of the list in 2019 with a consumer satisfaction index of 92% for the Model 3, which has thus become the most loved car in the U.S., just slightly ahead of the Porsche 911.

Tesla's customer-service structure is minimal, and most of its mechanics work out of trucks that go directly to the customer's home. Most of the problems, moreover, are diag-nosed – and even solved – remotely thanks to the vehicles' constant wireless connections with the factory.

Even though work on the cars is rare, some Tesla owners are not happy with the wait times. This is probably explained

The Tesla shop in Yorkdale Mall, Toronto, Canada. With the shift to online sales only, just a handful of Tesla stores should remain open in high-traffic locations in the future.

by the relative scarcity of Tesla service centers, which are mainly in large cities only. The company has set an aggressive timeline to fix the issue in North America and Europe since 2018. With Tesla's growing popularity we can only hope for better geographic coverage!

It is easy to understand the problems that the major automakers face if they want to compete with Tesla on its own playing field. Revamping their sales networks would cost colossal sums and entail in-depth transformation of their entire distribution strategies. What is more, is such restructuring feasible, given that sales account for only 28% of a dealer's turnover, with the rest coming from scheduled maintenance, oil changes, and replacing mufflers, brake pads, and so on? It is almost impossible for traditional automakers to switch to a "factory store" or "online" model, because they are so tied contractually to their own distribution networks. For example, the dealers alone have the right to make changes to their customers' cars. Consequently, updating a car's software directly and wirelessly is impossible without triggering an outcry from the dealers. Tesla will thus keep this important advantage over all its rivals for years to come.

The supercharger network

Various charging networks are spreading through Europe and the rest of the world. However, we must point out the automakers' lack of involvement in these networks, except, of course, for Tesla, which does nothing like everyone else. Tesla understood right off the bat that making a network of fast chargers available to its customers along major thoroughfares would eliminate the fear of running out of power once and for all. Tesla is constantly boosting its network, which consisted of more than 1,400 locations worldwide with over 12,500 super-chargers at the end of 2018 and hundreds more planned for the coming months. The map of planned installations completes the cover in the U.S. and in Canada as well as almost every country in Europe and Asia.

Tesla knows its products and can thus manage its fast-charging stations in its users' interest. That is an important competitive advantage over the power distribution grids that are also setting up charging stations. For example, Tesla charges its users for the minutes spent hooked up to a charging station if charging is complete! That obviously encourages the drivers to free up the spots quickly for the next users. Tesla also bans commercial vehicle fleets, such as cab companies, from using its superchargers. That is yet

A Tesla fast-charging station in Arlington, Texas.

another action to give priority to travelers on long trips who really need to "fill up!"

Tesla supercharging stations are easy to spot with their big red-and-white posts. That keeps their parking spots relatively free from ICE cars, whereas those of the other networks' less-readily-identifiable fast chargers are very often "squatted" by non-electric vehicles. What is more, Tesla charging stations often have eight, or even more, spots, which greatly limits the risk of finding them all occupied.

Tesla is also installing a large number of "destination chargers." This is a network of slower but more numerous chargers for recharging at night or during the workday, with the clear added aim of freeing up the fast supercharger spots for long-haul travelers.

Having the maker of your car as your energy supplier is obviously an advantage. So, the navigation screen on the dash shows you not only your route, but also where and when you should stop to recharge, and even the optimal recharging time to reach your destination. Here, once again, Tesla is the only automaker in the world to provide such a perfectly integrated service.

The gigafactory

Electric cars will still cost a pretty penny in 2019. Even without an advantageous cost price per mile, the purchase price of an electric car remains a great hurdle for the public at large. Tesla has thus banked on controlling the complete battery manufacturing chain from the very beginning. To ensure the numbers foreseen for 2019 and the following years, Tesla has partnered with Panasonic to build a huge lithium-ion cell manufacturing and battery assembly plant.

This gigafactory is located in Nevada, close to the California border. Once it is finished, it will cover 1,500,000 square meters or more than 16 million square feet! Tesla has announced that it will manufacture about 100 GWh of lithium-ion batteries, or more than 40% of global production. This huge facility is not outsized, however, for Tesla's planned output for 2019 is about

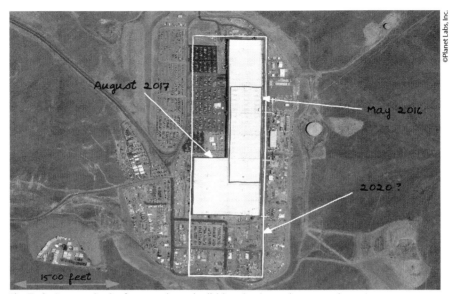

August 2017

May 2016

2020?

1500 feet

The Tesla-Panasonic gigafactory where the lithium-ion batteries are made.

350,000 to 450,000 cars, meaning that the factory will have to produce at least 35 GWh (450,000 x 77 kWh) , a volume most experts agree has already been reached. By the end of 2019, the future Tesla Semis will – in theory – start to roll off the assembly lines in large numbers, too. Each will require 1 MWh in batteries, meaning 1 GWh for 1,000 trucks. If we add stationary batteries, sales of which are rising from year to year, to this total, the gigafactory is more than warranted.

The gigafactory's mass output combined with technological advances will reduce the cost of Tesla batteries 30% by 2023.

Maximum factory automation

Tesla is innovating in manufacturing, too. Unlike traditional automakers, which rely on dozens of subcontractors, Tesla makes almost all its car parts in its own factories in Fremont, California, and Nevada (for the batteries). Extremely advanced automation has made it possible to ramp up production: Tesla has become, in just a few years, one of the biggest buyers of robots in the world.

The Tesla plant is extremely automated.

Tesla and the financial markets

Tesla is growing strongly, with turnover up 68% in 2017 and up 82% in 2018. The company's income has risen 62% each year on average for the past six years, three times as fast as Amazon's and five times as fast as Google's. However, as Tesla's main objective is growth rather than short-term profit, all of the money that comes in is immediately reinvested. Investment expenditures are rising and revenue is following with a lag. The shareholders who bet on this newcomer to the automotive industry and its innovative strategy have invested billions of dollars in what could become the leader of electric mobility. This risk-taking has been rewarded by huge capital gains, with the price of a Tesla share rising from less than US$40 in 2013 to US$250 to US$350 in 2018.

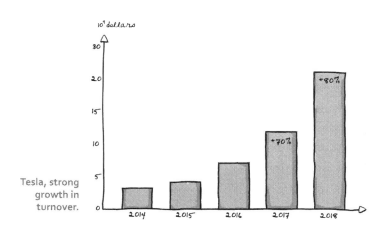

Tesla, strong growth in turnover.

The Tesla Roadster expected in 2021.

Since Tesla is focused more on long-term growth than on short-term profit, its stock-market value is being buoyed up by confidence in its future. The financial risks for Tesla are thus sizable: In the event of a big setback, such as a product that is rejected by its public, shareholder confidence and thus the cash at its disposal in the short term could suddenly dry up.

Tesla has consequently bet on the future to improve its finances quickly: The make's future vehicles can be reserved two years in advance with a substantial deposit. The sums taken in via hundreds of thousands of deposits on the Model 3 (a deposit of €1,000 in Europe, US$1,000 in the U.S.,

The Tesla Semi expected to hit the road in 2019/20.

and CAN$1,000 in Canada) and hundreds of deposits on Semis ($20,000) and Roadsters (US$50,000 in the U.S., €43,000 in Europe) since the end of 2017 have enabled Tesla to reduce calls for fresh financing while keeping its reputation for innovation at the highest level. It is even possible to reserve "Founders Series" Semis and Roadsters by paying the full price with your reservation: US$200,000 (€170,000 in Europe) for the "Founders Series" Semi and US$250,000 (€215,000 in Europe) for the "Founders Series" Roadster – and all that with at least a two-year wait before delivery!

The Model 3, the Tesla of 2018

The Tesla Model 3, with its base price of US$35,000, is the first Tesla designed for the public at large. This five-seat sedan is presented as a very serious rival of the BMW series 3 and Audi A4. Its highly streamlined body (CX of 0.21), vast glass roof, and no-frills interior hide unequaled technological advances.

The Model 3 is an extremely reliable car, with a range of 220 mi (240 or 325 mi as an option) and acceleration from 0 to 60 mph in 5.6 seconds (down to 3.2 s for the performance version), LED lights, and constant Internet connection. The car has a 4-year or 50,000-mile warranty and the drivetrain, battery included, is guaranteed to give at least 70% of its initial capacity after 8 years or 100,000 miles, even

©Tesla

By February 2019 a total of 200,000 Model 3's had been produced over 18 months.

The Model 3's minimalist interior.

120,000 miles for the long-range model. The Long Range and Performance versions have four-wheel drive systems with one motor in the front and one in the back.

Even without the luxury of Tesla's "Autopilot" or "Full Self-Driving Capability" software options, the driver of a Model 3 has all the equipment needed for 100% autonomous driving, *i.e.*, external cameras, radars, object sensors fore and aft, steering and brakes that can be controlled automatically, etc. Unlike conventional cars, all of the automotive functions are piloted by a 15" touch screen in the middle of the dashboard and two small joysticks on the steering wheel. The screen is used for everything, from displaying the car's speed to setting air vent orientation. And there's no screen behind the steering wheel!

Tesla Model 3

Available now in North America, Europe, and China.
Minimum price without options and various bonuses:

Standard version: US$35,000.
Standard plus version: US$37,500.
Long-range version: US$44,500.
Long-range AWD version: US$48,500.
Performance version :   US$59,500.

The other automakers

The major automakers cannot allow themselves to make as strong and unconditional a statement as Tesla, for various reasons: Their ICE car production plants cost billions and have yet to be fully depreciated; their research and development budgets are those of mature companies, not of technology startups; and, finally, a quick transition to electricity requires in-depth restructuring.

In the United States the makes at the head of electric and plug-in hybrid 2018 car sales are already known for their progressive image. Taking only full electric vehicles into account, you will find the three Tesla models trusing 80% at the top of the market (3, X, and S in that order) then the Chevrolet Bolt (7%) and the Nissan Leaf (6%), followed by a distant BMW i3 (3%). All the other accounted for less than 1% each.

In Europe, before the arrival of the Model 3, Renault-Nissan and Volkswagen were neck and neck at the top, with BMW close on their heels.

Even though the Model 3 is drawing closer and closer, the Nissan Leaf remains the global best-seller. More than 300,000 are already being driven all over the world. While the Tesla Models S and X are the rock stars of electric cars, they are not within everyone's budget. And while the Model 3 is starting to take to the road, the Leaf remains its most serious rival with the 2019 edition, which has a more pleasing look for all and sundry and a range that has been boosted to 226 mi (360 km) thanks to its 62 kWh battery.

Note. In the following paragraphs, the characteristics, options, and prices of the various models can vary from one country to the next, just like the various tax incentives, rebates, and bonuses. Nothing beats stopping by a dealer's or consulting a make's local website to get the right information.

The
Chevrolet
Bolt

Chevrolet Bolt

The Chevy Bolt was a commercial success as soon as it was launched in 2017, in both the U.S. and Canada. To create their first EV based on a dedicated platform, General Motors teamed up with LG, which designed the electric drivetrain in Korea. The Bolt received the prestigious "2018 Canadian Green Car Award." The Bolt was distributed in Europe under the Opel Ampera-e name in 2017 and 2018 but GM ended its European operations by selling the German brand Opel to the PSA (Peugeot-Citroën) Group.

The Bolt is a five-door subcompact hatchback, weighing close to 1.87 U.S. tons (1,700 kg) and powered by a 200 hp (150 kW) electric motor. The battery stores 60 kWh of energy, giving the sedan an EPA-estimated range of 238 mi (380 km). One-pedal driving is possible and the regenerative braking is even very easy to modulate by means of a little paddle at the steering wheel that controls the power of the electric braking.

Chevrolet Bolt 60 kWh

Two Bolt trim levels are available: LT and Premier. The latter offers more creature comforts, surround vision, and a lane change alert. Minimum price excluding options and various bonuses:

Chevrolet Bolt LT: $37,495 MSRP[1]
Chevrolet Bolt Premier: $41,895 MSRP

DC fast charging is a $750 option.

1   MSRP, also called sticker price, is the car manufacturer's suggested retail price

Fast recharging at 50 kW is possible, but if you are limited by a 7 or 3 kW wall box, a full charge will take 8 or 16 hours. Recharging on a 110 volt socket is recommended only as a last resort, as it would take more than a day to charge an empty battery fully.

Nissan Leaf

The Nissan Leaf is the Renault group's most popular electric car. With an eight-year track record and over 380,000 units already sold, the Leaf can claim the title of the most popular electric car in the world. Its sales have been rising steadily – slightly more than 50,000 were sold in 2017 – but the time had come to give it a makeover. That was done with the "model 2018" version, which has a range of up to 151 mi (250 km) in actual use. Its more generally-pleasing style, the increase in power to 100 kW (147 hp), and bigger battery (increased from 30 to 40 kWh) should continue to keep its sales figures in the upper percentile. The Leaf even became the best-selling car on the Norwegian market in 2018 – not "best-selling electric car" but "best-selling car," period, regardless of type of propulsion. The 2019 version, dubbed the "Leaf e+," has a 62 kWh battery and a powertrain output increased to 160 kW (214 hp). The EPA-estimated range is now 226 mi (360 km). The Leaf e+ is available now in the U.S.

©Nissan

The Nissan Leaf has opted for a more conventional look in 2018.

V2G-connected cars can truly serve as buffers for the grid by accumulating energy during periods of overproduction and returning it to the grid during high demand or an outage. In future, electricity providers will pay the users who contribute to the power grid through V2G systems.

Nissan's take on the V2G concept: Powering your coffee machine with your car in a power outage.

The Leaf's advantages include, under the code-name "e-Pedal," an energy recovery function when the accelerator is released. Intelligent driving assistance is also available as the ProPilot and ProPilot Park options. In such cases, the car is equipped with four high-resolution omnidirectional cameras and twelve short-range ultrasonic sensors. Moreover, these new features won it the prize for the best innovation for smart cars and self-driving systems at the CES motor show in Las Vegas.

The 2018 and 2019 Leafs are currently the only electric vehicles equipped with a bidirectional charger and the V2G function. In practice, that means that the Leaf can serve as an emergency standby battery for the power grid to which it is connected.

The Leaf's battery has an 8-year or 160,000-km warranty. Recharging is done at home on a standard 3 kW outlet or Type 2 socket 7 kW wall box. Fast charging of up to 70 kW is also possible with the ChaDeMo socket.

Nissan Leaf 40/62 kWh

Minimum price excluding options and various bonuses:
Leaf S 40 kWh : $29,990 MSRP
Leaf S+ 62 kWh : $36,550 MSRP

Add $6,000-$8,000 for various options, including ProPilot Assist, navigation, premium audio, etc.

The
Hyundai
Ioniq

Hyundai Ioniq and Kona EV

Ioniq. The South Korean automaker Hyundai has released
its new front-wheel-drive Ioniq with three types of engine,
namely, hybrid, plug-in hybrid, and electric motor. The electric Ioniq has an 88 kW (118 hp) permanent-magnet motor
under the front hood with the electronics module. The 28 kWh
battery is air-cooled and equipped with a preheating system.
It is located under the rear seat and the floor of the trunk. IIts
EPA-estimated range is 124 mi (200 km), which corresponds
to consumption of 13.3 kW/100 km – (or 4.51 mi/kW), one of
the lowest ratios on the market. The Ioniq's total efficiency is
excellent because of its very aerodynamic profile (Cx= 0.24)
and aluminum hoods.

The Ioniq's noteworthy features include the fact that its aux-
iliary electric system is powered by a 12 V lithium-ion battery
instead of the traditional lead batteries that are still found

Hyundai Ioniq 30 kWh

Minimum price excluding options and various bonuses:
Ioniq Electric : $30,315 MSRP
Ioniq Electric Limited : $36,815 MSRP

The Limited trim includes leather, navigation, and Automatic Emergency Braking (AEB) with pedestrian detection.

far too often in electric cars derived from an ICE model, for weight savings of 27 lb (12 kg). The heating and air-conditioning use a heat pump that can recover the calories emitted by the electronics module, which is a very appreciable advantage when temperatures hover around 0 °C. The level of energy recovery on deceleration is easy to adjust by means of two paddles behind the steering wheel, which makes one-pedal driving more comfortable. The warranty covers 5 years and 60,000 mi (100,000 km) for the car and 10 years (8 years in Canada) and 100,000 mi (160,000 km) for the drivetrain, battery included.

Kona EV. Hyundai unveiled its little SUV, the Kona, at the Geneva 2018 Motor Show in two versions offering 40 kWh and 64 kWh of storage. Its interior is very technological with Android and Apple connections and a head-up display (HUD). The announced ranges for these two versions are 180 mi and 281 mi (300 and 470 km), respectively. The Kona is nimble and fast with a power output of 150 kW (201 hp) and is available in three trim levels. DC Fast charging is possible at up to 100 kW so you may regain 80% of the battery capacity in 54 minutes.

The Hyundai Kona won the SUV of the Year award at the 2019 Detroit auto show. The Kona landed in Canadian dealerships in January 2019.

The Kona EV availability is even lower than for the Ioniq and the demand looks greater, so it is not unusual for dealers

©Hyundai

The Hyundai Kona

Hyundai Kona 64 kWh

Minimum price excluding options and various bonuses:

Kona SEL : $36,450 MSRP
Kona Limited : $41,150 MSRP
Kona Ultimate : $44,650 MSRP

in California to add a $5,000-$8,000 markup over MSRP. And buying a Kona in other CARB states or on the East coast should not be easy...

Kia Soul EV

The Kia Soul EV is a small, compact crossover that has the same drivetrain as the Hyundai Ioniq for an obvious economy of scale, since the two Korean makes belong to the same industrial group. Given its markedly squarer cross-section and length of 163 in. (4.10 m), the Soul EV is clearly designed for city driving. The motor has an output of 81 kW (109 hp).

It has fewer intelligent driving options than the Ioniq, however: There is just the LDA (lane departure alert) and automatic headlight management. Like all Kias, the Soul EV and its battery are under warranty for 10 years or 100,000 mi (160,000 km). The warranty covers all components, including the electric motor, battery pack, and Onboard

©Gshurley

The little electric crossover Kia Soul EV.

127

Charger (OBC), and remains valid for subsequent owners. The car is well thought out for cold weather, with a heat pump for heating the interior and the possibility of pre-heating the interior and battery before departure when it is connected to a power supply.

Fast charging is done via the ChaDeMo connector in the front. Recharging at home with the Level 2 charger incorporated in the vehicle takes 5 hours with a 240 V/32 A line.

Kia Soul 28 kWh

The EV+ trim adds fog lights, leather, and ventilated front seats. Minimum price excluding options and various bonuses:

Kia Soul EV : $33,950 MSRP
Kia Soul EV+ : $36,945 MSRP

Volkswagen e-Golf

Volkswagen has great ambitions on the electric mobility market and promises to come out soon with a complete range of vehicles based on the future all-electric MEB platform, including the I.D. (intended to replace the e-Golf) in 2020 and the minibus I.D. Buzz in 2022. Between now and then, the maker is concentrating its efforts in Europe on the e-Golf and, to a lesser extent, its little sister, the e-up! In the rest of the world, VW is investing the most massively in China:

©Volkswagen

The MEB platform will be the basis of all future electric VWs starting in 2020 (here the 2-motor 4-wheel-drive).

Blue-edged LED headlights make the
Volkswagen e-Golf distinctly recognizable.

©Volkswagen

That is where the MEB platform derivatives should generate the biggest turnover in the coming years.

The Volkswagen e-Golf has all the advantages of a conventional Golf, including its sturdiness, good grip on the road, and impeccable finish. To this it adds all the expected features of an electric car. Since its structure is that of an ICE front-wheel drive, the maker has simply replaced the engine-gearbox unit with an electric motor-step-down gears-electronic controls combination that is bolted into the same place. The battery, for its part, is placed under the rear seats. An experienced eye is needed to tell a Golf from an e-Golf. Aside from its badge on the trunk, the electric version has specific, almost completely solid rims; LED headlights with blue edges; and C-shaped LED front daytime running lights. To minimize manufacturing costs, Volkswagen has thus chosen to have only a strict minimum of parts that differ from those of a conventional Golf.

Like all Volkswagens, the e-Golf comes with a huge range of options. It is regrettable, in fact, that the heat pump that makes it possible to limit the drop in range due to heating in winter has been included in the options.

Volkswagen's Car-Net application is a definite plus: It lets you use a mobile phone to check the car's position and status, order charging and preheating, and call emergency services automatically if an accident occurs.

The e-Golf has been a great success since its roll-out in 2014, but it has made even more gains since 2017 thanks to a motor increased from 84 kW (115 hp) to 100 kW (134 hp) and a new 35 kWh battery (up from 24 kWh), which gives it a range of 200 km (120 mi) under real driving conditions. An e-Golf can be recharged fully at home in under 6 hours on a 7 kW three-phase socket or in 17 hours on a conventional 220 V 16 A socket.

Since the e-Golf is connected with a Type 2 or CCS socket, you can restore 80% of its range in just 45 minutes with the CCS socket of a fast charger. It should be pointed out that in some countries the charging cable for home sockets and CCS cable for fast charging are in the list of options.

Volkswagen e-Golf 35 kWh

The e-Golf is avalable in some U.S. states and in Canada. Minimum price excluding options and various bonuses:

Base SE: $32,790 MSRP
SEL Premium: $39,790 MSRP

BMW i3

BMW Group – owner of the BMW and Mini brands – announced that it delivered more than 140,000 electric or hybrid cars between 2013 – the i3's first year on the market – and 2018.

BMW has great ambitions for the electric car niche, with 25% of its cars slated to be electric or hybrid by 2025. The "i" range will not be used for the future self-driving cars, however. The next models expected to hit the market are the Mini Electric and iX3 SUV in 2020, and the self-driving iNext in the fall of 2021. A number of BMWs are already available as hybrids, such as the 330e and 530e and even the SUV X5 40e.

The compact i3 sedan, designed from the start on a specific platform, is BMW's standard-bearer. Its most amazing feature

The BMW i3, with its carbon fiber shell and antagonistic doors.

is its very narrow rear doors that open in the opposite direction to what is usual to make it easier to get into the back seat.

It is very rigid due to a carbon fiber body, has an excellent grip on the road, and the motor that drives the rear wheels eliminates all risk of wheel slip on starting. Its 33 kWh battery gives it an EPA-estimated range of 114 mi (183 km). The 2019 model and its 42 kWh battery now extend that by 33% to 153 mi (246 km).

There is also a "series hybrid" model equipped with a range extender ("REx"), *i.e.*, a small two-cylinder gasoline engine inherited from a BMW scooter coupled to an alternator, that extends the range by 80 mi (133 km) thanks to a 2.3 gal gas tank. Since 2019, the REx is no longer available in Europe. However, it is still an option in the U.S. The S version is another variant that is touted as more dynamic and better equipped.

BMW i3 120 Ah (42 kWh)

Minimum price excluding options and various bonuses:

BMW i3 120 Ah 170 hp :	$44,450 MSRP
BMW i3 120 Ah 170 hp w/Range Extender:	$48,300 MSRP
BMW i3S 120 Ah 181 hp:	$47,650 MSRP
BMW i3S 120 Ah 181 hp w/Range Extender:	$51,500 MSRP

The Jaguar i-Pace is European Car of The Year 2019

Jaguar i-Pace

This high-end sports model designed by Ian Callum for the Jaguar-Land Rover (JLR) group is made by Magna-Steyr, the plant that manufactured the Aston-Martin Rapid not long ago, in Austria. The i-Pace has been available at dealerships in the U.S. since Nevember 2018.

With a 90 kWh battery and four-wheel drive powered by two 147 kW (200 hp) motors, it has a total of 400 hp "under the hood." Under real conditions, it should have a range of about 300 km (180 mi). The i-Pace qualifies for the $7,500 federal tax rebate, an advantage now partially lost by Tesla and GM. As it is a luxury vehicle, i-Pace sales have not been overwhelming, with around 600 vehicles delivered during the first four months of U.S. availability.

Jaguar i-Pace 90 kWh

The "First Edition" 2019 variant is a more luxurious limited offer painted in a special "Photon Red" color.

Minimum price excluding options and various bonuses:
Jaguar i-Pace: $69,500 MSRP
Jaguar i-Pace First Edition: $85,900 MSRP

Soon ...

Most of the major automakers have announced new partly, mostly, or fully electrified ranges in the past few months, but almost all of these versions are slated for 2020 or later. Consequently, only a few new electric models are awaited this Year. The Audi e-Tron is a case in point.

The future Audi e-Tron Quattro should be available in late 2019.

Audi e-Tron Quattro

Audi has been working on its version of an electric SUV for three years and the end result appeared in its dealers' showrooms at the start of 2019 in order to compete with Tesla's Model X. With its three motors – one in front and two behind – the e-Tron should prove very agile thanks to fine control of the power sent to each wheel. The battery stores 95 kWh and the motors have a combined output of 300 kW (408 hp), even 503 during a brief boost. Its announced theoretical range is over 248 mi (400 km) in the WTLP cycle. It has been possible to reserve one in certain countries since early 2018.

Porsche Taycan

The Taycan, formerly known as "Mission E," will offer 440 kW (600 hp) of electric power and be available sometime in 2020 with a price tage of around $75,000 for the bare-bones version.

The Porsche Taycan is based on this Mission-E prototype.

Thanks to its 800-volt system, the Taycan's battery is supposed to charge from zero to 80% in just 15 minutes. The German carmaker has signed a deal with Electrify America to give Taycan drivers an unlimited amount of charges.

At home in China...

The Chinese government's new incentives for renewable energy sources and NEVs (the Chinese are very taken with the term "New Energy Vehicles") have had a spectacular effect on the supply of electric cars in China over the past year. The Chinese put more than 1,250,000 electric vehicles and plug-in hybrids on the road in 2018, which is more than half the global effort. However, one third of those EVs are low-quality, low-speed microcars that do not really compete with passenger cars as we know them.

Controlling global warming is not the priority in China, where most electricity comes from highly-inefficient coal-fired plants, but the Chinese government is pursuing two objectives in parallel: reducing pollution, which exceeds critical levels in its cities alarmingly, and bringing its car industry to the fore by taking advantage of the major foreign automakers' inertia and high import duties.

©Xinhua/Zhang Guojun

The Chinese NEV industry is booming. Here, the Yudo π 1 electric SUV assembly line in December 2017.

Since 2010, in the wake of very stringent regulations, electric motorcycles and scooters have taken the country's major cities, such as Shanghai, by storm. Between 30 and 40 million electric motorcycles and bicycles were sold in China in 2018, and there are more than 200 million in circulation as we speak. The two-wheelers are for the most part powered by lead batteries but they are gradually switching to lithium-ion batteries. Currently, the price of an electric scooter does not exceed $500.

However, electric cars have been starting to appear on Chinese roads over the past two years. The Chinese Ministry of Industry published its pro-NEV program in September 2017, according to which 10% of new cars will have to be electric starting in 2019. After that, the quota will rise to 12% in 2020 and 20% in 2025. In parallel with this obligation, the government has confirmed that it wants to continue its sales bonuses and tax rebates until at least 2020 in order to send the following clear message: China needs radical measures to control pollution in its major cities, and the solution involves electric mobility.

To give the local automotive industry a maximum advantage, huge import duties discourage purchasing foreign vehicles. What is more, the tax incentives and exemptions on electric cars apply only to local output or vehicles manufactured jointly with a Chinese company. So, there is nothing astonishing in the fact that the Chinese hit parade of sales includes very few American and European models. Still, to be eligible for the tax exemptions, plants co-managed by BMW, Renault, Daimler, and other western manufacturers will be going on line in China in two years' time. The only foreign company building a fully-owned car factory on Chinese soil is Tesla, which is expected to sell its locally manufactured Model 3's and Model Y's from its Shanghai plant in 2020.

Up 126% a year

NEV sales in China thus very logically more than doubled between 2016 and 2017, when they were growing by only 20% a year in the U.S. and Japan and 40% a year in Europe. Despite lowered incentives, the electric car market share in China for January 2019 was 4.8%. The Chinese government expects annual NEV output to hit 2 million in 2020 and NEV sales to make up 20 percent of the overall auto market by 2025.

...and elsewhere

We must already keep a watchful eye on Chinese electric vehicles, for everything points to their intention to target Europe in addition to saturating their own market.

One Chinese electric car maker, BYD (Build Your Dreams), has already landed in Lancaster, a charter city in LA County, California. Its first U.S. based facility has already sold 300 electric buses to public transit authorities and private companies and has capacity to produce up to 1,500 electric buses a year. BYD is also planning service and maintenance centers across the U.S.

BAIC, Zhidou, BYD, and Geely

More than 100,000 electric cars are made and sold in China every month, and with a market share slightly over 4% in 2018, the numbers will only rise. The lion's share goes to four car makers that are practically unknown outside the

© Jengtingchen

A BYD Yuan in
Shanghai,
China in 2018

Middle Kingdom's borders, namely, BAIC, Zhidou, BYD, and Geely. Here are some brief descriptions of their most popular models.

BYD Yuan and e5. BYD sold more than 22,000 units of its e5 front-wheel-drive sedan in 2017 and increased its production capacity even more in 2018. Its 48 kWh LFP lithium-ion battery withstands abuse fairly well, but tends to discharge rather quickly when not in use. Its motor has a rated power of 80 kW (108 hp), but can deliver bursts of up to 200% of its rated power to obtain sharp accelerations if needed. It is thus quite suitable for intensive use, such as in taxi fleets, which make up the bulk of its buyers. With its five seats, under 15-foot length (14 ft. 8 in.), and a real range of close to 102 mi (270 km) in city driving, it is quite appropriate for such use. Its price before subsidies is ¥196 000, or about US$35,500.

BAIC EC180. The world's best-selling electric car in 2018 racked up 82,000 sales in twelve months. The EC180 is a small 12-foot-long, 55 hp crossover. It has a range on the order of 90 mi (150 km) and its 30 kWh battery can be totally charged in six hours on a 220 V home outlet.

The BAIC
EC180

The basic version costs 150,000 Chinese yuan, or about US$24,000 before subsidies.

Note. BAIC is a state-owned company; it is also China's biggest automaker. Its big boss attended the opening of the new "NEV Technology Center" in Beijing at the end of 2017, where he announced that BAIC would stop selling ICE cars by 2025.

Zhidou D2. The two-seater Zhidou D2, like its little sister the Zhidou D1, is a tiny city car with a small range of action. It weighs in at 24 hp, is 110 inches, and has a range of about 60 mi (100 km) powered by a 15 kWh battery. It comes with a very complete range of equipment, including a navigation system,

The
Zhidou D2.

various driving assists, and even a WiFi access point. More than 40,000 were sold in 2017, but that figure fell drastically in 2018 with only 15,000 units sold. The Zhidou D2's decline is a confirmation that microcars are rapidly losing their appeal among the Chinese, mainly because China is scaling back subsidies for electric vehicles with a range under 180 mi. Before subsidies it costs around ¥152,000 (US$19,500.)

Geely Emgrand EV. With a length of just over 14 feet, the Emgrand EV has five seats but sacrifices a bit of trunk space to house its 45 kWh battery. It has two separate connectors, one for slow charging from a home outlet in 14 hours and the other for fast charging at 60 kW. The electric motor generates 95 kW (129 hp) and its range under real conditions is on the order of 120 mi (200 km). The car is warrantied for 60,000 mi (100,000 km) or 4 years, and even 5 years on the motor, electronics, and battery. Sales price excluding rebates: ¥250 000, or about US$39,000.

Note. Geely has great global ambitions, for in less than two years the company has bought Proton in Malaysia, Volvo and Polestar in Sweden, Lotus, and the London Electric Vehicle Company, which makes the famous black London cabs that have now been converted to electricity. Geely hopes to achieve a 90% NEV (electric and hybrid vehicle) production quota by 2020. In Europe Geely intends to start by launching electric versions of the Volvo V40 and XC40, based on the future CMA (Compact Modular Architecture) platform developed jointly by Geely and Volvo.

The Geely Emgrand

Trucks and buses

Coaches, buses, and trucks make up only one of ten vehicles on the road but account for about 40% of their CO_2 emissions. Besides producing considerable amounts of greenhouse gases, they are responsible for emitting more than a quarter of the gaseous pollutants that affect our health. Their low efficiencies when their big diesel engines are turning at low speeds, typically in cities and traffic jams, and are a major cause of the high fine-particle and NOx concentrations in the air. Heavy vehicles, *i.e.*, trucks and buses, are thus a major cause of the high prevalence of asthma and other respiratory diseases seen in the low-income populations on city outskirts and in the narrow streets of city centers. Electric propulsion could change this situation radically.

Just a few years ago no one was truly thinking about mass electrification of trucks for the simple reason that the batteries that they would have needed were not affordable. However, as we have seen, battery prices have been declining steadily and their performance has constantly increased, so much so that we heard some earth-shaking announcements in 2017. First of all, in China, BYD – the world's leading electric bus manufacturer that long remained under the radar in the West – continued on its roll. Next, the announced

©BYD

One of the municipal bus depots in Shenzhen, China. All of the city's 16,359 buses run on electricity.

market releases of electric semis by Tesla, Nikola, Kenworth, and others have raised real hope of seeing cleaner air in our cities a few years from now.

BYD buses

China was the first country in the world to make large-scale investments in electric buses. This took the shape of its "Ten cities, one thousand vehicles" campaign to promote electric buses that was launched in 2009. In 2016 alone some 80,000 electric buses were put in service. Twelve major Chinese cities have decided to stop using ICE buses by 2025 at the very latest, led by Shenzhen, with a population of 12 million, just north of Hong Kong. Shenzhen is the seat of the world's biggest manufacturer of electric buses, BYD. The company thus very naturally supplies almost the entirety of the city's bus fleet. So, Shenzhen has become the first city in the world to have converted 100% of its fleet (16,359 buses) to electricity. In the course of the last few years, the city has put 300 chargers into service in its bus depots and installed 8,000 lampposts fitted with charging sockets near its bus stops, with each charger capable of recharging a bus's battery pack fully in two hours. Shenzhen justifies its over-$500 million investment by the reduced running cost per mile and above all the improvement in the city's air quality. At the end of 2018, all 22,000 taxi cabs in the city were also replaced by electric models. The transition was so fast that the lack of charging stations is creating tension between taxi drivers.

The Tesla Semi

Tesla's announcement of its truck project, the Tesla Semi, shook the world of transport. The fact that it is electric is not what triggered amazement, but rather its performance levels, and, even more, this 36-ton tractor-trailer's price/performance ratio. Not only does it accelerate like a sports car, but above all it has a range of 480 mi (800 km) at 60 mph (100 km/h) and can zoom up 5% grades without dipping below 60 mph. Its maintenance costs are reduced below those of a conventional diesel truck for the same reasons as pertain to electric cars: ultra-simple mechanics and energy-recovery braking that spares the brakes. For the truck, Tesla has also planned to eliminate another cost item, namely, replacing the windshield. This is a frequent and expensive operation in conventional semis. It is avoided for the Tesla Semi by the use of ultra-resistant "thermonuclear" glass.

Given its announced price of US$180,000 for the "480-mile range" version, which is only 25% more expensive than a diesel truck of the same size, the offer is impressive. Despite the fact that it will be available no earlier than Christmas 2019 and a US$20,000 deposit must be put down, reservations are piling up on Tesla's sales counter. All the major companies want to test a few as soon as possible. The list includes Pepsi, UPS, DHL, Walmart, the Norwegian Postal Service, the Canadian supermarket chain Loblaws, the Italian Fercam, and even the brewer Anheuser-Busch. Tesla also gives buyers the possibility of reserving the deluxe version produced in the limited "Founders Series" for US$200,000, but those interested must pay the full price of the truck as the deposit.

It is obvious that the interest in an electric truck is predicated above all on its low operating costs or cost price per mile (CPM). By replacing diesel fuel with electricity and capping maintenance at very low levels, the Tesla Semi should have a CPM of less than 80 cents, or 20-30% less than those of its diesel rivals. This advantage, combined with a manufacturer-guaranteed lifespan of 1 million miles, amply justifies the success it has had to date.

Some simple calculations done with some known figures enable us to estimate some important parameters regarding the Tesla Semi that have been carefully omitted in the official press release, such as the outputs of its motors and price of its battery. The lack of official figures is justified because the vehicle has not yet been officially approved.

In the following table the estimated values are given in italics. Although they have not been confirmed, they are logical in

The Tesla Semi.

light of the announced performance levels and price. Most impressive is the battery's cost price, which, at US$75/kWh, is below the predictions that the highest-profile analysts gave a year ago for...2025! If these values are confirmed, they announce an incredibly low cost price per mile for all electric vehicles starting in 2020, or at least for those that Tesla will make! The first Tesla Semis should be seen plying the roads in the first half of 2020 in North America.

Tesla Semi characteristics	Value ( ) : long-range version
Sales price	US$150,000 (US$180,000)
Range	288 mi/480 km (480 mi/800 km)
Acceleration from 0-100 km/h (0-60 mph), empty	5 seconds
Acceleration from 0-100 km/h (0-60 mph), loaded	20 seconds
Charging time for 400 km/240 mi	35 *min* (30 min)
Number of motors (identical to that of the Model 3)	4
Cruising speed ascending a 5% grade	65 mph
Power consumption when loaded	1.9 kWh/mi (1.2 kWh/km)
Warranty, battery excluded	1,000,000 mi/1,600,000 km
Cost price per mi (CPM)	US$0.88
Power	*1,000 hp*
Battery capacity	*600 kWh (1,000 kWh)*
Charging power	*500-1000 kW*
Battery's cost price	*US$75/kWh*

The Nikola One hydrogen truck

The Nikola One

The Nikola One truck manufactured by Nikola Motor of Salt Lake City, Utah (USA), was announced at the end of 2016. It will be propelled by an electric motor powered by a fuel cell backed up by a 320 kWh battery. Its 1,000 hp output, combined with a huge range (from 780-1,200 mi/1,300 to 2,000 km), makes it a tempting proposition.

The Nikola One should be available starting in 2020 or 2021 in North America for US$375,000 or US$5,000-7,000/month under lease-purchase agreements. Two lighter trucks, the Nikola Two and Nikola Tre, are also planned both in hydrogen and battery variants declined in 500kWh, 750kWh and 1MWh versions.

Despite the attractiveness of the proposition, the Nikola must solve several problems in the relatively short term, not the least of them being to find enough capital to ensure production. The Nikola Ones will also require service stations that can deliver sufficient amounts of hydrogen, and just a few dozen such stations exist in the U.S. Nikola will thus have to finance the construction of a distribution network with its own money. Nikola's aim is to manufacture 5,000 trucks a year to start off and up to ten times as many in the longer run.

The Lion8

The Québec-based Lion Electric Company has launched its Class 8 electric urban truck, Lion8, which will be marketed in the fall of 2019. Lion Electric Co is broadening its vehicle offering after selling electric school buses in North America and its May 2018 launch of an electric minibus adapted to the requirements of school and public transportation. The Lion8 is designed from the ground up to be electric and has a range of up to 250 miles (400 kilometers) thanks to its 480 kWh battery. The Lion8's engine power reaches 350 kW (470 hp). The truck weighs 11 tons on its own, while its weight with cargo is up to 25 tons. The Lion8 is said to offer 80% energy cost reduction and 60% operational cost reduction. And, as usual for electric vehicles, the truck's components require very little maintenance, thereby keeping the total cost of ownership to a bare minimum. The first truck will be delivered to SAQ (Société des alcools du Québec), a Quebec-based liquor retailer. The price has not yet been revealed but pre-orders are already possible with a CAN$5,000 deposit.

©The Lion Electric Co

The Lion8 class 8 urban truck was unveiled in March 2019 by the Canadian company The Lion Electric Co.

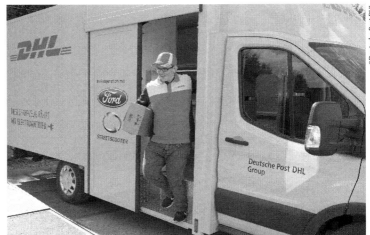

The Ford
StreetScooter
Work XL
electric
delivery truck
designed
with DHL-
Deutsche Post.

Delivery trucks

The major automakers have already starting testing the "zero emission truck" waters, but almost all of them have decided to tackle the market with smaller models, especially those designed for door-to-door deliveries in town or public services such as mail distribution and garbage collection.

Ford-DHL. The distribution company DHL, which owns the German mail service Deutsche Post and has long been known for its global warming mitigation efforts, has joined forces with Ford Europe to build and put the StreetScooter XL into service. This utility vehicle is derived from the popular Ford Transit. It has a loading volume of 20 m^3 and easy access from the back as well as via a long sliding side door. Its battery stores 30 or 60 kWh of energy and gives it a range of 48-120 mi (80 to 200 km).

The vehicle has been in production in Germany since 2017, with the first ones intended for Deutsche Post, which has been a pioneer of electrification in its country. Indeed, Deutsche Post already runs a fleet of 3,000 small electric trucks and more than 10,000 electric scooters. According to Ford Europe, each StreetScooter Work XL will save close to 500 US gal (2,000 liters) of diesel fuel and 6 metric tons of CO$_2$ emissions a year.

©Daimler-Mitsubishi

The Mitsubishi
eCanter
e-delivery truck
is perfect for
urban deliveries.

Daimler-Mitsubishi. The German automaker intends to launch a complete range of electric utility vehicles in 2019 and is already starting to distribute its Fuso eCanter. Small-series production of the Fuso eCanter began in Portugal in late 2017 and the truck has a real range of 60 mi (100 km) and can carry a payload of 2-3 metric tons. It is easily identified by its LED headlights and running lights. Its 129 kW (180 hp) motor is powered by an 82 kWh battery.

The first 150 units were delivered in 2017 to DHL and a few other delivery companies that are testing it in Amsterdam, Tokyo, New York, and Lisbon. Large-scale production should begin in late 2019.

Volkswagen. Not satisfied with attacking the passenger-car market, Volkswagen has also turned its attention to delivery

©Volkswagen

Volkswagen's
e-Crafter
delivery van.

vans. The e-Crafter is thus the first-born electric model of its "Truck & Bus Division," which is known for its Man and Scania brands. The e-Crafter has a 43 kWh battery that gives it a range of more than 72 mi (120 km) in real situations (120 mi/200 km according to the theoretical NEDC).

Hybrids and hydrogen

6

There are more and more hybrid cars on our roads. The combination of an ICE and an electric motor gives them certain advantages over each separate means of propulsion. Unfortunately, they also inherit the drawbacks of the two solutions. Ecologists see in the hybrid merely a way to extend the reign of fossil fuels. Automakers see in them a way to improve performance and reduce their cars' CO_2 emissions so as to be able to comply with increasingly stringent regulations. Finally, in which direction do they actually tip the scales?

Plug-in or not?
Parallel or series?

Hybrids. A hybrid that is not a plug-in, such as the iconic Toyota Prius, is a gasoline-powered car whose engine is mounted on the same axis as an electric generator motor. The two are said to be "mounted in parallel." In the hybrid car, the ICE engine is the normal means of propulsion, but during descents or deceleration the car's kinetic energy is recovered by the generator, which stores it in a battery.

The electric motor then draws on the battery during low-speed travel or to boost acceleration in order to add its contribution to that of the ICE.

Hybrids can at best travel a few miles at moderate speed in electric mode. They usually have an electric propulsion system that works at 48 volts to minimize risks. Their strong points include the great ease of restarting the ICE in Stop & Start mode, with the electric motor operating as a starter. Hybridizing the means of propulsion improves the ICE's mileage, but all of the energy used by a hybrid car comes from the fossil fuel in its tank.

© EurovisionNim

The hybrid Toyota Prius charges its battery only when it is moving.

Plug-in hybrids. Plug-in hybrids follow the same plan, but the battery is usually slightly more powerful and can be recharged at home like that of a full electric car. The electric circuit for propulsion is seldom at 48 V, as for the non-rechargeable hybrids; it is more in line with electric car design and operates at high voltage: 250 V or more.

These cars can be considered short-range electric cars with large backup ICEs. As in the case of pure hybrids, energy recovery through braking helps to save fuel consumption. PHEVs (plug-in hybrid electric vehicles) can drive up to 30 mi (50 km) in electric mode on one battery charge. After this distance, the ICE wakes up and takes over. The

The BMW 530e iPerformance, a plug-in hybrid. The charging socket flap is visible on the left wing.

driver can choose to drive on the gasoline engine, with an empty battery, until reaching the garage, or to use the ICE to recharge the battery, burning fuel to do so. The latter solution can be useful if you are driving back into town after a long trip, because the electric mode is much more economical in city traffic.

An example of the PHEV is the BMW 530e iPerformance. Its 4-cylinder 184 hp gasoline engine is assisted by a 70 kW (95 hp) electric motor. The buffer battery is 9 kWh and the car's theoretical range in electric mode is 29 mi (46 km). Its standardized fuel efficiency, according to the NEDC guidelines, is 30 mpg solely because the test cycle gives priority to low-speed travel. Its CO_2 emissions thus officially do not exceed 79 g/mi (49 g/km), which makes it very attractive in many countries where registration tax and annual tax are based on emissions.

Series plug-in hybrids. The series hybrid is actually an electric car onto which a gas-powered electric generator has been grafted, making it possible to recharge the battery if necessary. The typical example of a series hybrid is the 2018 BMW i3-Rex (REx = Range Extender). It is the same vehicle as the electric BMW i3 with an alternator entrained by a 650 cc 34 hp two-cylinder engine inherited from a BMW scooter in the trunk. Hybridizing the i3 adds 264 lb (120 kg) and $3,850 to the price. In exchange, the 2-gallon-tank adds 78 mi (130 km) to its range, and the tank, we might add, is easy to fill.

Ⓐ Electronics module   Ⓒ Battery
Ⓑ Electric motor   Ⓓ REx

The electric and "series hybrid" versions of the BMW i3,
The Rex (range extender) is a 650 cc 2-cylinder engine linked to an alternator.

Mixed hybrids. The "mixed hybrids" category makes the most of the advantages of series and parallel hybrids. The drivetrain can be reconfigured and operate in parallel hybrid mode, in which the electric motor assists the ICE. However, it can also run like a conventional electric vehicle while its ICE powers a generator (different from the motor) that recharges the battery.

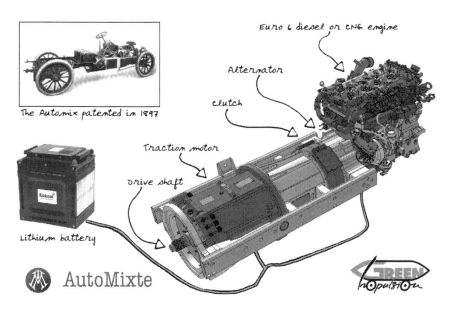

The Automix patented in 1897

Euro 6 diesel or CNG engine

Alternator

clutch

Traction motor

Drive shaft

Lithium battery

AutoMixte

The AutoMixte® mixed-hybrid drivetrain for buses and trucks by Green Propulsion.

The mixed hybrid's greater complexity means it is reserved for heavy vehicles such as buses and trucks. On the other hand, its more flexible operation lowers its operating costs below those of its diesel competitors in cases where full electric mode is not – or not yet – the best solution. The Belgian company Green Propulsion sells this type of drivetrain under the "AutoMixte®" brand (the pioneering manufacturer that was already making hybrid cars around 1900).

The plug-in hybrid – a transitional role

The average U.S. motorist drives less than 30 mi (50 km) a day. Most PHEVs can make such trips without relying on an ICE. They thus behave most of the time like an electric car. However, only one in five new buyers of an electric car opts for a hybrid instead of a "true" electric car. Why?

Hybrid car buyers are usually motivated by the desire to shrink their environmental footprints. They want to get tax rebates, but are not yet ready to go to full-electric cars. Various reasons explain that, such as the fear of too short a driving range, prices that are still too high, but above all too small a range of cars that does not include their ideal vehicles. Indeed, the 2019 models do not yet include an electric SUV or large family vehicle, except for the Tesla Model X, the price of which remains a deterrent for the bulk of the population.

Plug-in hybrids are transitional objects between two eras. Their reign will be short and their role limited, but without them automakers will not be able to meet their commitments to reduce the CO_2 emissions of their mid-range models. As transitory solutions, plug-in hybrids have a positive influence on electric motor take-up:

- The owners of hybrid vehicles learn to appreciate "full electric" driving;
- they learn to use the chargers and charging networks and to fill up at the pump less often;

- most of them install wall boxes in their garages;
- they become accustomed to planning their trips according to range;
- more than half of them intend to buy an electric car after the hybrid;
- without hybrids, automakers would not be able to meet the CO_2 emissions standards imposed by states adopting California's rules or in Europe;
- the automakers and dealers get used to selling and maintaining electric components such as batteries; and
- parking lot, shopping mall, and restaurant managers feel the demand more and more, which motivates them to extend the network of available charging points.

Hybrid pros and cons

For: It is easy for automakers to adapt an electric motor and small battery to their existing models.

For: Hybrids are eligible for numerous tax advantages in almost every country. In the U.S. plug-in hybrids are eligible for federal level incentives, typically $3,000 to $4,500. This advantage is nevertheless being challenged in a number of countries.

For: The hybrid eliminates the anxiety that is linked to the car's range and the gradual deterioration of the battery, even if long trips are rarely taken. Only in town is the hybrid more economical.

For: By increasing demand for batteries, sales of hybrids help to lower their prices.

For: Given the hybrid's small battery, the hybrid car market is less likely to suffer from a possible future cobalt supply crisis or problems procuring other metals used in electric vehicles.

For: Plug-in hybrids are or will probably be accepted in future low CO_2 emissions areas. In France, hybrids are entitled to "Crit'Air 1" stickers allowing them to operate in restricted traffic zones ("ZCR" in French), many of which are already in effect.

Against: A hybrid is more expensive and complex than the ICE model from which it is derived.

Against: There is a huge difference between the theoretical EPA efficiency and the actual value. Most hybrids have EPA mile-per-gallon city estimates in the 30's to 50's (best-case-scenario), values that are not really representative of real-life conditions. Not a single hybrid on Earth burns as little as the 70 mpg or so announced.

Against: Once it leaves the city, the hybrid very quickly switches to its ICE. The driver enjoys its advantages in urban areas only.

Against: Some hybrid car buyers content themselves with the tax rebates they get and never take the trouble to recharge their batteries. That results in reduced efficiency and a risk of damaging the battery.

Against: There is often less space available than in the basic model. The less bulky electric drivetrain does not translate into more roominess.

Against: A small battery means moderate electrical power, so that you do not get the punch of an electric start and the amount of energy recovered on braking is limited.

Against: Hybrids cannot take rapid chargers.

Against: Hybrids must still make regular visits to the gas station.

Against: The resale value of hybrids is uncertain, even though they are resold quickly because they are relatively rare. And since, starting in 2020 or 2021, the cost of using an electric car will be markedly below that of using an ICE car, second-hand price trends remain a real unknown.

Should you buy a PHEV?

If you are tempted by a hybrid because it meets your needs better than an electric car, don't hesitate to weigh the pros and cons and, most important, to borrow the model you're considering in order to test it on your usual routes. Don't forget to take the cost price per mile truly driven into account. That means allowing for your annual mileage, depreciation, any tax rebates available, and the number of years that you hope to use the car.

Should you buy it just for the tax advantages?

Plug-in hybrid electric vehicles are eligible for bonuses and tax rebates in many countries and regions. However, many users who are aware of the fact that many PHEVs have a full-electric range of just a few dozen miles buy them simply to benefit from such discounts, but then never connect them to the socket. Why take the trouble of doing so to save just two dollars at the start of the day? To keep the battery charged, the driver then activates recharging via the ICE, and the car's energy consumption skyrockets to about 13 mpg at peak speeds and 19 mpg on average instead of the 30 mpg announced by the manufacturer, who of course calculated the figures according to the EPA standard and used a fully-charged battery.

Buying a plug-in hybrid and never plugging it in is a very poor plan. Once the purchase incentives are a thing of the past, you'll find yourself with a heavier, more complex vehicle that is less efficient and more expensive to use and maintain than a simple non-rechargeable hybrid. There is even the story of the buyer who asked the dealer to keep the "useless" charging cable because it would simply take up space in the trunk!

For the 2019 models, there is a tendency for governments no longer to subsidize "fake hybrids," that is, those that have a tiny battery and thus little electric range. In Quebec, for example, the capacity of your battery must be at least 4 kWh for you to be eligible for a "Drive Green" subsidy. The amount of the discount depends on the battery's capacity and can rise to 500, 4,000, or 8,000 Canadian dollars. Careful, though: The high-end vehicles that cost more than CAN$75,000 are not eligible for this bonus. In some European countries, the hybrid will have to embark a minimum battery capacity to benefit from deductions.

And the fuel cell in all this?

The subject inevitably comes up again when talk turns to electric cars: "What about the fuel cell? Is it going to replace batteries or not?" While it is true that fuel-cell vehicles (FCVs) exist, their advantages and drawbacks are very poorly known. Let's take a tour of the subject.

Hydrogen and fuel cells

A fuel cell is a small chemical reactor with two electrodes (an anode and a cathode) and a separating electrolyte. Hydrogen gas is pumped into the anode and oxygen into the cathode. The chemical reaction between the hydrogen and oxygen produces electricity, water, and heat. Since the voltage of a hydrogen cell is very small, on the order of 0.7 V, a large number are piled together, giving a "stack" of fuel cells that is nevertheless referred to as a cell. As a large portion of the energy carried by the hydrogen is lost as heat, a fuel cell has a yield of about 50%.

Hydrogen is a very light gas. To supply the fuel cell with a sufficient amount, a hydrogen-powered car must store it in a tank under very high pressure, typically 700 bars. This tank is made of aluminum surrounded by a thick layer of very tough carbon fibers. The Toyota Mirai's tank contains 5 kg of hydrogen, takes up 4.6 ft^3 (125 liters) of space, and weighs more than 200 lb (87 kg).

On exiting the tank, the hydrogen goes through an expansion valve to bring its pressure down to a usable level, which means warming it. The hydrogen concentration determines the amount of current that comes out of the cell. In addition to the hydrogen tank, the cell needs oxygen. The ambient air is microfiltered and then compressed before being sent to the cell. The hydrogen cell's discharges are harmless: just a little water.

The fuel cell produces a huge amount of heat. A cooling system is thus needed, just as in a conventional car. This heat is used to heat the hydrogen's expansion valve and heating the car's interior is never a problem: Just as in an ICE car, the cooling water can heat the interior.

Why the battery?

Although the hydrogen fuel cell supplies enough current, a battery is added. This is indispensable for several reasons:

- It takes the hydrogen fuel cell several seconds to react when the gas influx changes. The battery makes it possible to start immediately when the traffic light changes without having to wait for the fuel cell to ramp up its power.

- The hydrogen fuel cell produces a current but cannot work in reverse and turn electricity into hydrogen. The battery is thus indispensable to store the energy recovered braking and going downhill.

- The higher its rated power, the more the hydrogen fuel cell costs. So, it is scaled according to the car's mean energy use, with the battery supplying the extra bursts of power needed to accelerate or go uphill.

Running on hydrogen in practice

On the road the FCV or "hydrogen car" is used like a conventional automatic car. It operates smoothly like an electric car and has a large range – 300 mi (500 km) or more. Moreover, its tank is filled at the pump in a just a few minutes.

Today, in 2019, the crucial problem of the FCV is the availability of hydrogen pumps. Public hydrogen pumps are found almost only in Japan (91 stations) and the United States (39 stations, all in California, according to the U.S.

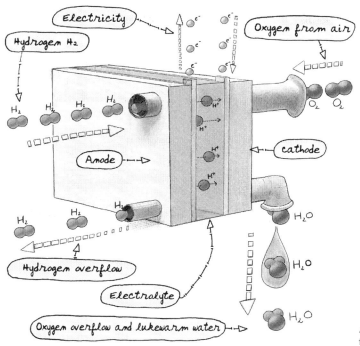

Electricity

Hydrogen H₂

Oxygen from air

H₂ H₂ H₁ H₂

Anode

H⁺

H⁺

cathode

H⁺

O₂ O₂

H₂O

H₂ H₂ H₂

Hydrogen overflow

Electrolyte

H₂O

Oxygen overflow and lukewarm water

H₂O

A hydrogen
fuel cell.

Department of Energy), with a few dozen more in Europe (there were 25 in 2016). The greatest hobble on setting up hydrogen filling stations is their cost, which is set at between 1 and 4.5 million US dollars, depending on the source, for a station able to fill up ten to twenty cars a day, that is, a daily output of 220 lb (100 kg) of hydrogen.

There are only three FCVs currently on the world market: the Toyota Mirai, Honda Clarity, and Hyundai ix35 FCEV. The Daimler group and its Mercedes brand launched an FCV project in 2013 but have since abandoned it. One manufacturer that was already the center of attention in 2018 is the aforementioned Nikola. This American company based in Utah proposes an electric truck, the 1,000 hp Nikola One, that is powered by a 300 kW fuel cell. With its 220 lb hydrogen tank, this 65,000-pound truck should have a range of 1,140 mi (1,900 km). Reservations are already being taken, with full production expected in 2021.

The Toyota Mirai FCV

Outside Japan, the Mirai FCV is available in California, Hawaii, and seven European countries. It has a 114 kW fuel cell and its buffer battery can store 1.6 kWh of electricity. There were slightly under 3,000 Mirais on the road in 2018.

Toyota announces a mean fuel efficiency of 79 mi/kg, which is equivalent to about 25 mpg in terms of stored energy, meaning a total range of more than 300 mi (500 km) for its two-part 5 kg tank. The car weighs 4,000 lbs and accelerates from 0 to 60 mph in 9 seconds.

The Mirai is priced at just $59,260 MSRP, from which various tax rebates must be deducted, but Toyota discourages outright purchases, preferring to lease the car at $349 per month with $2 499 due at lease signing. Toyota offers up to three years of fuel, capped at $15,000, upon buying or leasing a Mirai and the car is eligible for the CA HOV carpool sticker.

Where does the hydrogen come from?

Even though water contains heaps of hydrogen, pure hydrogen is not extracted from nature as oil and natural gas are. A large amount of energy is required to produce it. Hydrogen is merely a means of carrying energy in gaseous form rather than as an electric current.

Almost all the hydrogen in the world is extracted from natural gas – from methane – by means of a high-temperature, high-pressure distillation process called reforming. This reforming also produces CO and CO_2 and uses markedly more energy than can be recovered from the hydrogen produced.

Hydrogen can also be produced by electrolyzing water. However, that is anything but easy, because the oxygen and hydrogen produced by electrolysis tend to recombine spontaneously, creating a risk of explosion if the method is not well controlled. What is more, the yield is not greater than 60%. The amounts of hydrogen produced by electrolysis globally are thus tiny.

Is the hydrogen-powered car a hybrid?

Despite the common name of "fuel cell," intimating combustible fuel, there is no combustion or explosive reaction in a hydrogen-powered car. The hydrogen is not burned, serves only to carry the electrical energy, and is turned back into water at the end of the process. The fuel cell is the "receiving end" of the energy carried by hydrogen; it produces the electricity that is sent to the buffer battery and electric motor. The FCV is thus an electric car with energy stored in gaseous form rather than in batteries.

It can also be considered a series-mounted hybrid vehicle that combines two technologies: A conventional electric car with batteries and regenerative braking, and a hydrogen fuel cell that recharges the battery from its tank.

Transporting hydrogen

The hydrogen produced at low pressure must be stored in huge tanks or compressed at very high pressure to be taken to service stations. This compression step typically uses the equivalent of 20% of the stored energy. If you've ever seen a garage air compressor that compresses air at 10 bars to inflate tires, imagine the size of a 700-bar compressor! The gas gets very hot in the compressor and must thus be cooled, on pain of contracting later on and losing pressure in the storage tank.

The gas is then transferred from the production plant to a truck, from there to a filling-station tank, and finally to the car's tank. The gas expands at each transfer, causing cooling. The various valves must thus be warmed up to keep them from freezing.

From this we can understand that one of hydrogen's draw-backs is the low energy yield between production and consumption.

Pros and cons

Let's list the various advantages and disadvantages of a hydrogen fuel cell:

For: Large range and short filling time.

For: Like electric cars, no pollution from the car.

For: Hydrogen is well suited to heavy vehicles, planes, and ships, which use energy almost constantly for long periods of time.

Against: Hydrogen is not suited to light vehicles such as passenger cars, which use energy very erratically, especially in city traffic.

Against: Hydrogen's "well to wheel" energy capacity is low because each step in the production-consumption cycle involves large losses:

- Pumping methane from the ground: Only 91% of the energy in methane is usable, as 9% is used for the extraction itself).

- Transforming methane into hydrogen: 60% of methane's energy is found in the hydrogen produced.

- Transporting hydrogen: 80% of the transported energy remains available at the filling station.

- Converting hydrogen to electricity: The fuel cell's yield is 50%, with the other 50% of its energy lost as heat.

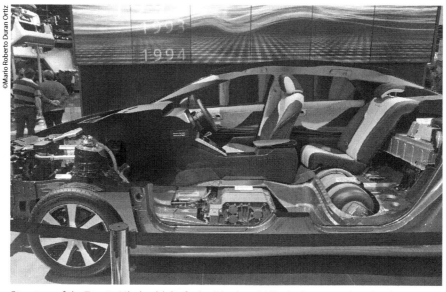

Structure of the Toyota Mirai, with its fuel cell in the middle, hydrogen tank under the rear seats, and 1.6 kWh battery in the trunk.

The
Toyota Mirai

- Converting to mechanical energy: The electricity generated is turned into mechanical energy to propel the car,
as in a battery-powered EV, with a yield on the order
of 85-90%.

If we multiply the successive yields observed for each step,
we end up with a total yield for the hydrogen fuel cell of only
21%. That is scarcely more than a quarter of the 80% for
a battery-operated electric car supplied with photovoltaic
electricity generated at home. Even for electricity from a gas-
fired power plant, the battery-operated EV has a calculated
efficiency, from "well to wheel," of 40%. Hydrogen compares
favorably only with the ICE and its total efficiency of 14%.

Calculated efficiency of the FCV: $0.91 \times 0.6 \times 0.8 \times 0.5 = 0.21$

Calculated efficiency of a battery-operated EV (gas-fired PP): 0.40

Calculated efficiency of a battery-operated EV (PV panels): 0.80

Calculated efficiency of an ICE car: 0.14

Against: The quasi-nonexistence of filling stations accessible to the public.

Against: The cost of the onboard system (fuel cell,
high-pressure tanks, pumps, coolants, etc.) is very high. It
would appear impossible, given its complexity, to reduce its
cost price to that of a battery-operated car. It is commonly
thought that the Mirai costs Toyota twice its sales price.

Against: The cost of a filling station capable of servicing twenty cars a day is currently $4.5 million (5-10 times the cost of a gas station). That is a major hobble on the distribution network's expansion.

Against: Producing hydrogen at home by electrolysis powered by photovoltaic panels may be possible in the future, but the technology required is not affordable today.

Against: Hydrogen is obtained from natural gas. Now, extracting natural gas contributes greatly to global warming for, even though the extraction produces little CO_2, huge amounts of methane — up to 50% of the gas pumped at certain wells — is lost into the air. And while methane disappears from our atmosphere in 12 years, *i.e.*, eight times faster than CO_2, its greenhouse-gas effect is 21 times that of the same amount of CO_2. Producing hydrogen is thus very far from ecological.

Who still believes in the hydrogen fuel cell?

Automakers have practically given up all hope of turning a profit on hydrogen fuel cells. The most active are the Japanese Toyota and Honda and South Korean Hyundai, which have slackened but not stopped their efforts completely, given the huge government subsidies that they get in Japan. Toyota's recent declarations in favor of battery-operated models confirm its growing disinterest in hydrogen, even though it is keeping the Mirai in its catalog.

European automakers have stopped investing massively in hydrogen for light vehicles in favor of the lithium-ion battery. BMW admits that hydrogen makes sense only for high-end vehicles and is keeping a development laboratory that plans to produce a very small series in 2021. Mercedes presented a "GLC F-cell" at the 2017 Frankfort Motor Show that combines a fuel cell and a rechargeable 13 kWh battery. A few GLC F-cell vehicles were delivered to selected customers in the German market at the end of 2018.

A hydrogen filling station.

Oil companies remain very interested, in contrast, for the fuel cell's development will enable them to expand their natural gas market. As stated above, natural gas is already serving to produce hydrogen as part of the gasoline and diesel refining processes. Oil companies would thus be open to reducing gasoline production in exchange for increasing hydrogen production.

A few innovative startups are working on original solutions that might one day overcome hydrogen's drawbacks. So, Hypersolar, a company based in Santa Barbara, CA, is developing electrolysis units that work directly with sunlight without using photovoltaic electricity.

The real problem with hydrogen

Ten years ago people imagined that fuel cells would be used on a large scale in ten years' time. Now that this period has elapsed, fuel cells continue to appear to be a possible solution in ten years. However, the hydrogen vs battery comparison has changed completely since 2009, when batteries cost more than $1,000 per kilowatt-hour, almost ten times today's price. The advantages and disadvantages of hydrogen have remained largely unchanged, whereas the lithium-ion battery has advanced on all fronts: better yield, better environmental conservation, 1,000% better performance, and much lower prices.

There continues to be a future for hydrogen fuel cells, but not in light vehicles, where lithium has won. Possible applications will be in heavy vehicles such as trucks and construction machines, ships, and, in the more distant future, aviation. The most promising initiative in the realm of trucks is the Nikola One semi, which should roll off the assembly line in North America in 2019.

The autonomous car

The electrification of transportation is going to upset our habits. And yet, that is but a small change compared with the revolution that will hit in the next five years, for the driverless autonomous car is about to arrive. Indeed, it already has, since various experiments are ongoing in several U.S. cities.

Lawn mowers first; now cars?

No one is astonished any longer to see an automatic lawn mower or robot vacuum cleaner going about its business on its own, literally letting sleeping dogs lie and avoiding the tricycle left lying about. Some cars on our roads can already use the steering and brakes to avoid obstacles, slow down in a bottleneck, or even zigzag around something. The high-end sedans made by Cadillac, Mercedes, BMW, and of course Tesla are intelligent enough to react to the unforeseen and their electronic brains are never caught napping.

Why think that these options reserved for deluxe models are going to upset our existence? Because the threshold for triggering a series of events will soon be reached.

Once a car is able to move without human intervention,

- if there is no driver, a driver's license will no longer be needed;
- if there's no driver, you can drink alcoholic beverages before taking your car;
- self-driving cars should cause 4-5 times fewer accidents than occur right now;
- car insurance premiums should plummet;
- trucking rates and cab fares should drop considerably;
- the professions of truck and cab drivers will eventually disappear;
- driverless taxis will be available everywhere and at all times;
- with very cheap taxis, people will buy fewer cars;
- with cab-sharing, transporting people will be almost free;
- with far fewer cars sold, there will be fewer cars on the road;
- the drop in car sales will cause automakers to go bust;
- there will be no more traffic jams;
- no more need to park, thus large areas will become available in cities for other uses;
- new activities will be created, based on an economic model in which short-distance transportation will be practically free;
- and that is just the start of what lies ahead!

Hundreds of analysts and transportation professionals are concerned about the autonomous car and its consequences, for millions of jobs and billions of dollars are at stake. The coming revolution is not visible to the public at large, so no one is worrying. That's logical, as automotive onboard intelligence does not change our lifestyles. At the very most, today, in 2019, we see media coverage or articles on small-scale tests. But in how much time will the curtain be raised for this new play? Some claim it will take ten or twenty years. Others believe that things will change by 2030, or even earlier. How can we judge for ourselves?

The Google-Waymo autonomous car with a supervisor who does not touch the controls. Notice the cone of sensors on the roof.

The history of the autonomous car

2000. The DARPA Grand Challenge is an off-road driverless car race launched by the U.S. Army. Not a single participant crossed the finish line!

2005. Another, more complex, DARPA Grand Challenge was raced over 132 miles. A team from Stanford University saw its car cross the finish line in a little under 7 hours.

2009. Google hired the 2005 Grand Challenge's winning team to work on its self-driving car project. This produced the Waymo company within the Google group.

2013. A Mercedes Class S drove itself over 60 miles of German roads. Nissan, Mercedes, and BMW announced autonomous cars for 2020. A number of Waymo test cars were released on California's roads with a supervisor behind the wheel who did not, however, touch the controls.

2016 (October). As of this date, all Tesla cars are equipped with a "hardware version 2" computer and enough cameras and sensors to be able to drive themselves once the necessary software becomes available.

2017. Six hundred driverless Waymo cars continue to test the new technology, but without a supervisor on board. They have already driven more than 300,000 miles on open roads without a driver at the wheel. Many partnership agreements are signed with the goal of running self-driving vehicle fleets, *e.g.*, between Google-Waymo and the rental company Avis, between Apple's Autonomous Vehicle Division and Hertz (another rental company), between General Motors and the operator of on-demand transportation Lyft, etc.

2018. The French company Navya's six-seat Autonom Cab shuttle becomes available to everyone in Paris first, and then other French cities. The user can call a shuttle via the system's mobile app, share the ride (or not) with other users, and control the door locks. A screen in the cabin enables users to monitor traffic and displays tourist information. Waymo announces ordering "thousands" of Chrysler Pacifica plug-in hybrids – 8-seat family cars – to fit them with sensors and start putting them on the road in a few major U.S. cities before Christmas 2019.

In 2017, Uber had a plan to turn 24,000 Volvo XC-90 plug-in hybrids into an autonomous taxi fleet to be put on the road between 2019 and 2021. But after a fatal accident in Arizona involving one of its cars and a painful lawsuit filed by Waymo, Uber cancelled its self-driving truck program in July 2018.

An autonomous Volvo XC90 plug-in hybrid tested by Uber in San Francisco.

2019. Waymo seems to be the most advanced company in the driverless car race. The company's back-up drivers in their test cars are less and less taking control in difficult situations. They are now correcting the vehicle course manually only once every 11,018 miles or so.

Tesla promise "full self-driving" features available before end of 2019. The system will offer "automatic driving on city streets" but warns that the currently enabled features require "active" driver supervision and do not make the vehicle autonomous.

Six levels of autonomy

Not all machines are equally intelligent. The U.S. National Transportation Safety Board (NTSB) classifies vehicles from cars without electronic assistance to driverless cabs according to the following six categories (based on the Society of Automotive Engineers' classification):

Level 0: No automation (the driver alone controls the driving).

Level 1: Driver assistance: A few assistance features exist, such as ABS (anti-lock braking system) and skid control.

Level 2: Partial automation: The vehicle can control the accelerator, brakes, and steering, but the driver must constantly pay attention to the driving. S/he may release the steering wheel temporarily.

Level 3: Conditional automation: The driver must be present, but does not have to watch the road at all times. S/he must be ready to retake control at all times and on short notice.

Level 4: High automation: The vehicle can drive itself in certain circumstances. The driver is indispensable outside these predefined cases and may retake control at any time.

Level 5: Full automation: The vehicle can drive itself in all circumstances. A driver is optional.

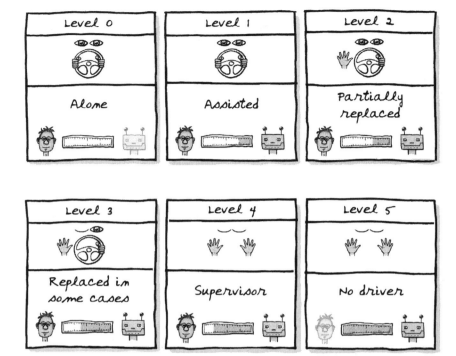

In the United States, Waymo autonomous cars are already driving at Level 5.

The EasyMile EZ10 driverless shuttle has already been deployed in 20 countries and has been in operation in Denver, Colorado since January 2019.

The 12-passenger EZ10 "Level 5" autonomous shuttle is programmed to make designated stops along predetermined routes and runs at an average speed of 15 miles per hour.

A faster S-curve than for the electric car?

Artificial intelligence techniques and the sensors manufactured today suffice to control driverless cars. Several forecasters, including the famous Tony Seba of Stanford University, think that if legislation is adapted by 2020, only ten more years will be needed (bringing us to 2030) for driverless cars to account for 95% of the miles driven in the U.S. and even in Europe. This revolution will definitely begin in big cities, where more than half of travel involves means of transportation other than the private car, before spreading to rural areas.

And why should we adapt so quickly? Very simply for economic reasons! The idea is that the entire transportation sector will change its economic model. We are going to leave the reign of the family car to enter that of "Transport as a Service" or TaaS, to use today's jargon. Getting rid of the car and replacing it with a mobile phone app that calls a driverless cab will save US$6,000 per household and do away with the need for new car loans. This miracle solution will free up close to one billion dollars for the North American population.

Take-up of the shared autonomous car should follow an S-curve like that of the electric car. This curve is starting now, at exactly 0% as 2019 began. However, given the billions spent by Google, Tesla, Lyft, and others, it definitely will not remain there. According to Tony Seba, take-up will be even faster than for the electric car because the end-users' potential savings are more immediate and much greater. Will the shared autonomous taxi

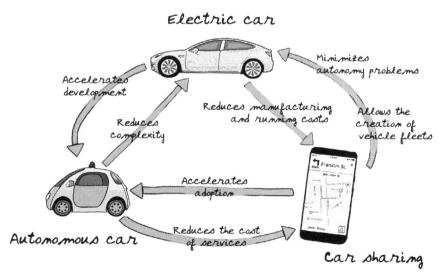

The virtuous circles of the autonomic and the electric car will reinforce each other.

revolution take place as suddenly as Tony Seba thinks, or do we wait until 2040 or 2050? It is too early to tell with certainty, but the first signs of change are starting to appear.

The greatest upheaval in store for us will be due to the fact that robot cars can drive all the time and be shared among several users. Today's cars are immobile 95% of the time. The idea is to send them out to work as taxis when a user doesn't need them, for example at night or while the user is at work.

"No driver" means "no need for rest breaks." We shall thus see shared autonomous cars doing 90,000 mi (150,000 km) a year or even more, going from user to user as soon as they've completed a trip.

In line with this new "TaaS" model, each robot car on the road will be able to replace 4-6 family cars, each of which does 15,000-18,000 mi (25,000-30,000 km) a year. They will be electric for obvious economic reasons and also because that will be the only solution for a car to survive doing more than 360,000 mi (600,000 km) reliably. The total number of cars on the road around the world will thus go from more than a billion to 250 million in just a few decades, whereas the United Nations forecast in 2013 that the global fleet of cars would reach 3 billion by 2050 (a prediction made before the autonomous car became plausible).

The huge drop in the number of cars will eliminate traffic jams, reduce the number of accidents, and thus leave commuters with more free time. Other virtuous cycles will play in favor of adopting the TaaS economic model. Consider the downtown areas, which, being no longer clogged with traffic, will attract potential buyers more easily, potential buyers who themselves will be very pleased to have more money to spend once they've given up their individual cars.

In the first chapters we imagined an S-curve for electric car take-up based on more or less the same number of cars sold each year. The electric car suddenly makes the advent of the autonomous car possible. The shared autonomous car will in turn give electric car take-up a strong shot in the arm. The two S-curves are inseparable and will reinforce each other.

Let's imagine...

2025. Uber, Lyft, Tesla, and Google put fleets of shared autonomous vehicles (AVs) into service at rock-bottom prices. They become the largest car buyers (except for Tesla, which makes them). Private individuals buy fewer and fewer cars.

2030. End-of-life cars disappear to be replaced by a much smaller number of electric cars. Autonomous-cab fleets compete ferociously with each other and take over the market. They are practically the only ones still buying cars. Robotization is everywhere on the roads. New unforeseen uses for robot cars arise, gradually replacing the enterprises that they have forced to close.

2035. The automobile fleet is halved (500 million instead of 1 billion on the planet), but 95% of the miles driven are driven by robot cars. The individual passenger car costs ten

The robot car with a thousand uses

The robot car will reduce local travel costs to such a point that dozens of new enterprises will spring up, if only to breathe new life into some old forgotten trades.

Three California startups – Nuro, Udelv, and Robomart – ascertained that the boom in online sales failed to include the fresh produce market. People want to see, feel, and choose their fruit and vegetables themselves.

So, Robomart and its emulators invented the grocery store 2.0, that is, a robot car equipped with shelves of fruit and vegetables, a card reader for payments, and route planning in the neighborhood, and a new store was born!

Robomart's autonomous grocery store delivers to your door and lets you choose your fresh produce.

times more. It becomes a rarity on the road. Only 5% of young people still get driver's licenses.

2040. The private car is used by no more than 1% of the population. Autonomous taxis are so cheap that the cost of an unlimited mileage pass is negligible. The private car with an internal combustion engine becomes a curiosity. It may not be sold or used in cities, but is an attraction nonetheless!

This scenario seems completely crazy today, but what about in a few years' time? Keep your eye on the autonomous car scene. Some big surprises may lie ahead!

The legal angle

Letting driverless private cars, shuttles, and trucks loose on the road is not imaginable without serious changes to the laws in effect. It should not take too long to convince our governments to take action, because they, too, could find in such driverless transportation fairly inexpensive solutions to a number of thorny problems. The lawmaker's role includes providing behavioral guardrails to ensure the people's welfare and safety. The autonomous car will indeed make it possible to clear our cities' clogged streets without having to change the road infrastructure. It should also reduce the number of traffic accidents without requiring new investments.

The U.S. Department of Transportation (DOT) has published its vision of safety in the NHTSA document *Automated Driving Systems 2.0 — A Vision for Safety*. It states very clearly, "… automated vehicle technologies possess the potential to save thousands of lives, as well as reduce congestion, enhance mobility, and improve productivity. The Federal Government wants to ensure it does not impede progress with unnecessary or unintended barriers to innovation," meaning no legal barriers. "Safety remains the number one priority for the U.S. Department of Transportation (DOT)…" Thirty-three of the fifty states already have laws and regulations on the books allowing the use of automated driving

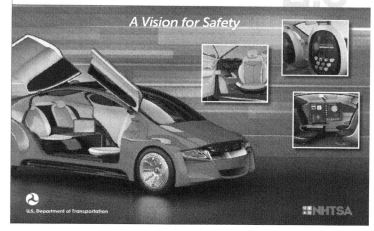

AUTOMATED DRIVING SYSTEMS

A Vision for Safety

©NHTSA

U.S. Department of Transportation

NHTSA

The NHTSA (National Highway Traffic Safety Administration) publication *Automated Driving Systems 2.0 — A Vision for Safety* (DOT, USA).

systems (ADSs) on public roads under certain conditions. The federal government allows testing under a special regime of exemption from certain safety rules but imposes various limits, such as the number of vehicles on the road, which currently may not exceed 2,500 per manufacturer. At the request of Google-Waymo and General Motors-Lyft, this limit could be raised to 100,000 very soon.

Almost all countries in Europe have ratified the 1968 Vienna Convention on Road Traffic, Article 8 of which stipulates,

- "Every moving vehicle or combination of vehicles shall have a driver;" and
- "Every driver shall at all times be able to control his vehicle..." and have his hands on the wheel.

The Vienna Convention on Road Safety is currently being amended. It already stipulates that automated driving systems will be allowed on the road, provided that they comply with the UN's regulations on vehicles and can be controlled, even deactivated, by the driver if need be. Once the final text is adopted by the European authorities, the Member States will have to adapt their respective traffic codes accordingly.

Belgium is one of the first countries to have taken these legal matters into its own hands by publishing, in 2016, a "code of good test practices" for pioneering companies. This code subjects self-driving vehicles to a 30 km/h (18 mph) speed limit on public roads and provides for the presence of a person on board who can take control of the vehicle if necessary.

Germany adopted a similar regulation in 2017, but replaced the speed limit with the obligation to install a "black box" in the vehicle to serve as a witness in the event of an incident or accident.

In Canada, and in Quebec in particular, while tomorrow's legislation is still in flux, the autonomous car is already a thing of the present. The research institute FPInnovation launched a driverless shuttle project with Motrec International in 2017. The first shuttle's wheels are expected to start turning in 2020.

According to a study by the international auditor KPMG called *2018 Autonomous Vehicles Readiness Index*, the Netherlands, Singapore, U.S., Sweden, UK, Germany, and Canada are the countries best prepared for the arrival of the autonomous car, and in that order.

And insurance?

The matter of liability in the case of an accident with a driverless autonomous car is not simple. Like the manufacturers, insurers are convinced that the autonomous car will reduce the number of accidents, since statistics show that close to 90% of traffic accidents are due to human error. In North America alone, more than 35,000 fatalities and ten times more accidents with injuries could be avoided each year representing savings of $5 billion for the authorities. Insurance companies are thus taken with the idea, but will have to adapt. If a driverless car is found liable for an accident, this liability will most likely be borne by the vehicle's manufacturer or the supplier of the software that controls it. Road infrastructure, parking lots, and cab services will also see changes in their insurance contracts.

©General Motors USA

Production of the future Chevrolet Cruise for shared-vehicle fleets should begin in 2019. Notice the numerous radar and lidar sensors on the roof and absence of a steering wheel and pedals.

We are thus heading for fleet insurance policies where the insured will be the manufacturers or, in some cases, shared-vehicle fleet managers. Several car manufacturers, such as Daimler-Mercedes, Tesla, and Volvo, have, moreover, already announced that they would like to manage their own shared-vehicle fleets themselves.

With most traffic consisting of shared autonomous vehicles, insurance will no longer be attached to the user, or even to the owner, but to the vehicle itself.

The owners of cars with a level of autonomy greater than 1 can already benefit from specific coverage, usually at more than 25% below normal rates, from certain insurance companies.

What if the autonomous car is not shared?

Mobility experts see the dawning of an era of shared autonomous cars with pleasure. However, one of their great fears is that the autonomous vehicle will be a success but no one will want to share theirs! In this case, many people will be tempted to use their own cars to get about, even if they have to cope with city traffic jams, because they'll take advantage of not having to drive in order to work or busy themselves otherwise without having the impression of wasting their time.

If, thanks to the autonomous car, running costs drop and the barriers to using or owning a car (age, driver's license, drinking, state of health, etc.), disappear, the number of vehicles on the road could triple between now and 2030! Imagine a car that drives you to work in the morning while another one drops the kids off at school and then picks up the grandparents for an afternoon in the countryside! It will be a world of congestion!

Luckily, the uncontrolled proliferation of autonomous cars is highly unlikely to occur. The new economic models and potential productivity gains will be too great to be ignored. The vicious circle of expanding urban thoroughfares should quickly give way to the virtuous circle of recovering the spaces freed by deserted parking spots. The advantages for private individuals and public authorities alike should greatly overcome reluctance to give up car ownership.

Abandoning your private car?

There are two main reasons why drivers will abandon the idea of replacing their current cars by new ones and turn instead to hailing autonomous cabs:

- First, trying the new scheme won't cost anything. There is no purchase to make, not even the tiniest deposit to put down, and neither commitment nor subscription. Just presenting a means of payment to the taxi's card reader will suffice.
- Second, the cost price per mile will be halved immediately and continue to drop thereafter, thereby widening the gap between the annual cost of a private car and that of an autonomous taxi with each passing year. Competition between operators to win market share will guarantee public prices almost identical to the cost price as long as no clear monopoly develops.

There are also some good reasons not to give up owning one's own car:

- Resistance to change: Why let yourself be controlled by robots when the existing solution has worked for more than a century?

©Gemma Longman

A traffic jam in Bangkok: This is what we can expect if we sidestep the autonomous car revolution.

- The possible wait times when you need a robot car unexpectedly and the risk of depending on outside elements that we cannot control (and are in the hands of Google, Lyft, Uber, and others).
- The possibility of buying an autonomous car for yourself becomes attractive when you know that you can make a profit by letting others use it for a fee, but only when you've decided it. This idea, which is implied in Tesla sales contracts, opens up some fascinating prospects.

The economic operators

Uber, like the other on-demand car-sharing providers, is acquiring market share thanks to a network of independent drivers. These drivers are helping to create an empire from which they will be excluded as soon as legislation allows it. Uber has polled its clientele and concluded that users prefer to do without a human driver if the service's safety and reliability remain the same. The avowed goal of these companies is to get the largest possible market share, not to make money. The huge amounts of capital invested in the service over the years is being converted little by little into a client base with maximum loyalty. Profits will start to be generated once the main expense – the car's driver – can be dropped from the equation.

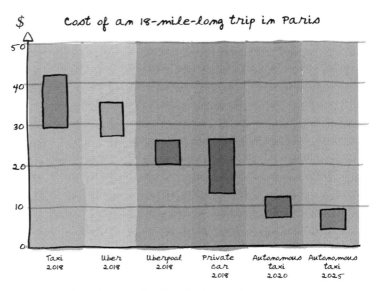

$ Cost of an 18-mile-long trip in Paris

Price comparison of an 18-mile trip in the Paris region.

As is the case today, the passengers will pay for their rides according to the distance covered. The various operators are expected to engage in a price war for years to come, and the users will be the first big winners of this cutthroat competition.

Automakers, for their part, will have to take up positions in one of the two possible camps: Either sell vehicles to the fleet operators (like Volvo, which is selling cars to Uber) or position themselves directly as renting out cars on demand. BMW and Tesla are in this second camp. The third option, that of "I do not believe there is a future for the autonomous car," will of course remain possible, but its partisans run the risk of finding themselves marginalized. The proponents of this third track include Mazda, which remains convinced that its position – "We make cars for customers who love to drive" – is solid.

The major automakers are in for financial upheaval with the emergence of the robot car: no more huge advertizing budgets, luxurious motor shows, and showrooms, for example. To sell cars by the thousand to fleet managers, they will have to canvas and convince a few well-chosen people. The public at large will no longer be involved. In contrast, software development, electronic sensor development, mapping, and testing will become the main cost items.

Guided by the desire to rationalize investments rather than pleasing millions of different users, automakers will probably opt for a smaller number of different models, which will facilitate in turn the extensive automation of their plants. The automotive industry will thus reduce its human workforce drastically in both factories and distribution networks.

Let's not lose sight of the fact that all of this will not happen overnight. The change will have far-reaching impact on our lifestyles but will take place gradually. So, private cars and driverless vehicles will have to coexist for many years. Both automakers and the public authorities will have to reconcile these two facets to enable users to make the best choices and automakers and "TaaS" operators to make enough money to grow, and all this without jeopardizing user safety. This will most definitely be an iterative process of trial and error. However, one thing is for sure: The decisions that are made in the next five years will have huge consequences for the future of the transportation industry.

The Tesla Model 3 – a driverless car in need of software

Tesla's latest addition is not a sedan like the others. It is equipped with all the sensors and motors need for 100% autonomous driving: two radars, eight cameras, and twelve ultrasound sensors. Even the basic version, without options, has all this kit! All the vehicle's controls can be remote-controlled electrically: The onboard computer commands not just the brakes and accelerator, but also the steering wheel, lights, charging-socket flap, seat and mirror positions, and even the orientation of the air vents on the dash board and opening of the glove compartment.

The Tesla Model 3 has no key. It is controlled by a secure mobile application.

The Model 3's stark interior was also designed from the start for driverless use with occasional passengers only. There are no dials or switches such as stud a conventional car's dashboard; the controls are accessed only via a large touchscreen mounted in the middle of the slab that replaces the dash. In "driverless taxi" mode, the screen can be used to display the multimedia content that the passengers desire with no risk of the passengers' hitting the wrong button and changing the car's operating settings inadvertently. Even entry into the car remains under the onboard electronics' control: There is no key to open the doors; a cell phone or swipe badge suffices. Consequently, clients who have booked a ride can identify themselves and open the car door with a simple tap on their cell phone's screen.

The onboard computer also has access to a wide-angle video camera that monitors the entire interior. So, in "robot taxi" mode, the Model 3 will be able to check whether the passengers are indeed out of the vehicle before starting again and heading for the next patron.

The only thing missing for the Model 3 to operate in this 100% autonomous mode is suitable software. It may be ordered as a US$5,000 option[1] at the time of purchase, but will be delivered only when Tesla finishes fine-tuning the

---

1 Tesla pricing information provided here was accurate in March 2019.

software and traffic regulations allow its use. Tesla is not putting forward any dates for either! Buyers who have chosen this option will probably have to wait many more months. As for those who preferred to wait and see, they will always be able to acquire the software afterwards, but at a higher price.

Pending the advent of this autonomous mode, the Model 3 owner can seek consolation in the US$3,000 "Autopilot" option, which corresponds, with a few exceptions, to Level 2 on the NTSB scale. Note that the autopilot option is mandatory before you add the "Full Self-Driving" option, meaning it is now possible to purchase a (soon) fully autonomous car for US$43,000 only.

The Tesla network

Tesla plans to activate – at an as-yet-unspecified date – its "Tesla Network," a fleet of driverless autonomous taxis. A portion of these vehicles will come from Tesla's "long-term rental division," but the owners of Teslas equipped with "Level 5" autonomous software will be able to contribute to the network, and be paid per mile for this! Imagine, for a second, that, as you sleep, your car slips out of the garage and spends the night earning its living as a taxi. As a Tesla owner you would have the additional choice of limiting the potential users of your car to your family or friends and to the times and days that suit you. Surprising, isn't it?

From a marketing standpoint, Tesla's idea is one of a kind. It will make it possible to sell luxury cars with the assurance that the car will pay for itself or, at the very least, reduce its annual budget by a sizable chunk.

No Teslas for Uber drivers

All Tesla car buyers undertake, in Tesla's sales contract, not to engage in remunerated car-sharing schemes, save in the Tesla network. This is stated explicitly on Tesla's website: "Please note that using a self-driving Tesla for car sharing and ride hailing for friends and family is fine, but doing so for revenue purposes will only be permissible on the Tesla Network."

Tesla network users. The Tesla network will function very similarly to Uber's. The user will use a mobile app to call a car, s/he will receive a confirmation along with the vehicle's time of arrival, and her/his account will be debited in proportion to the miles covered. A recent study estimates that the price of a ride in an autonomous Tesla Model 3 should not exceed 60 cents per mile, or about one-third to one-half the price of the car-sharing services of Uber, Lyft, and others. To ensure complete geographic coverage, Tesla will put in service in various places the number of cars necessary in the areas where the supply from network participants is short of the mark.

What should we think of all that?

While a large number of people have already heard talk about the autonomous car idea, less than 10% of the population is aware of all the implications that it could have on our lifestyles. The people with above-average knowledge, for their part, waver between excitement over a promising technology and deep skepticism.

A recently-conducted poll in the U.S. shows that half the motorists questioned state that the steering wheel will have to be pried from their dead hands before robots replace everyone. Only the respondents under 25 thought they would see the reign of robot cars and disappearance of the driver's license in their lifetimes.

Autonomy Levels 3 and 4 will garner the most success. It does indeed appear that the great majority of motorists are in favor of adopting automatic features that improve safety, but not if they have to give up all control. One-third of the poll's respondents, without distinction to age, added that they would never buy a "Level 5" autonomous car.

©Nicolas DUPREY

The EasyMile's EZ10 autonomous ten-seat shuttle will run only on predefined routes, but routes that are open to everyone.

Finally, in a study targeting the users of shared cars in major U.S. cities, a majority (56%) of those surveyed said that they felt more at ease in a car driven by a human being than by a robot.

Most experts in the sector, cab drivers and fleet managers included, do not see autonomous cars being adopted massively before 2030. However, everyone concurs that the automotive industry will have to show clearly that this new technology is safe, reliable, and economical before the public at large adopts it.

Controversies, arguments, and predictions

8

There's nothing like a conversation over cocktails (at a motor show?) to bring up the topic of "electric cars." After five minutes you will have heard all the arguments listed below, almost equally divided between those who are "for" and those who are "against." Here, then, are the elements you need to keep the ball rolling as you wait for the dinner bell.

The electric car is a flop because...

...it is too expensive

An electric car costs 20 to 60% more than its ICE counter-parts. The lower cost price per mile offsets the difference only for those who can pay out a large sum as of the initial purchase. However, this difference should narrow in the next two to three years. Thereafter, the trend should even reverse: In 2025, the purchase prices of electric cars will be at least 10% cheaper than those of equivalent gasoline-powered models.

...it is not really available

Automakers propose very few electric models. However, affordable electric models will start appearing in all segments, including large family cars and pickups, between 2019 and 2020. Most major automakers have announced the complete "electrification" of their ranges by 2025.

...the ranges are too limited

Most electric cars have true ranges of only 90 to 180 mi (150 to 300 km). The fear of running out of power far from a charging station puts off many potential buyers. However, this drawback is going to lessen a little more each year because of the fast-growing network of charging stations. In the case of new vehicles, steadily declining battery prices are enabling automakers to offer less and less restrictive ranges. So, Nissan increased the range of its Leaf from 22 to 30 kWh in 2016, and to 40 kWh in 2018. Even better, the 2019 e-Plus version offers 64 kWh, allowing for a 226-mile (364 km) EPA-estimated range. In the Tesla corner, the now available $35k base Model 3 delivers a 220-mile range. As we can see, the electric car's driving range will soon be almost on a par with those of its ICE counterparts.

...charging takes much too long

A third of North America's population looks askance at electric cars because they take so long to charge. It is true that it takes hours to charge a battery fully at home, whereas filling up at the pump takes just a few minutes. However, you seldom have to charge a battery from 0 to 100%.

Average gasoline car	North Dakota	Washington	Norway
g CO2/mile 360	357	54	5

CO$_2$ emissions of an average gasoline car in the U.S. (25 mpg) and an equivalent electric car recharged in North Dakota, Washington, and Norway where 98 % of the electricity comes from renewable sources.

An electric car is usually recharged at night, when the charging time has little importance. A quick recharge along the way proves necessary a few times a month. That is when the charging time counts. Superchargers, of which there are still too few, let you recover 36-54 mi (60-90 km) of range in a half-hour. This situation will improve in the coming years thanks to increasing numbers of fast-charging stations and more powerful batteries, but there is still a long way to go.

...no benefits for the fight against global warming

Close to 25% of the car drivers believe that driving an electric car produces as much greenhouse gas emissions as a diesel engine. But is it true? Actually, it isn't! Even though internal combustion engines have made undeniable progress and have better and better fuel economy, their energy yields are still disastrously low. Electric propulsion remains 30% more effective, even, *i.e.*, when sourced from fossil fuels. In Quebec, where electricity is more than 97% renewable, the context is among the most favorable in the world. In the U.S., Washington is number one, with over 70% of its electricity coming from renewables, mostly hydropower.

...it uses metals that are rare and mined unethically

The EV's batteries contain lithium and cobalt. These metals are not truly rare, but are available under economically profitable conditions in only a few places in the world. There are millions of tons of lithium in seawater, but extracting it would be too costly. Lithium is recovered from the salt flats where it is much more concentrated, such as on the high plateaus of South America. Cobalt is more problematic, because half of the world's cobalt is located in the Democratic Republic of Congo (DRC), a politically unstable country. Part of this cobalt – called "gray sector cobalt" – comes from mines controlled by militias that are hostile to the government. These mines undergo no official inspections and are notorious for their deplorable working conditions as well as for using child labor. Their output is slipped into the official mines' outputs by underhanded means. As a result, investigations, trials, and disputes often block up to 10% of the country's cobalt output for long periods of time.

Even though these problems concern only 5% of global cobalt production, they are disturbing nevertheless. The big client companies, led by Apple and Tesla, are thus making efforts to procure cobalt outside the DRC and investing in mines in the U.S. and Canada. The best way to solve the problem would be to do without cobalt completely. A large proportion of battery research is thus focusing on cobalt-free chemistry.

...it, too, generates fine particles

The electric car also emits fine particles. Where do they come from? From brake wear, of course! The brakes are subject to wear and the matter of which they are made ends up as particles in the air we breathe. This argument is valid, but applies to ICE vehicles as well, for they also have brakes and thus the same drawback. The only difference is that electric cars use their brakes to slow down a lot less because of energy recovery. That is why their brake pads are still virtually intact after 120,000 mi (200,000 km). So, the argument is founded, but so weak that it can be forgotten.

...it costs the government a lot

Is the electric car subsidized? Yes. Outrageously subsidized? Not really. In the U.S., the federal government and a number of states offer tax credits for lowering the up-front costs of EVs. The federal Internal Revenue Service (IRS) tax credit amounts to $2,500 to $7,500 per new EV purchased for use in the U.S. but this tax credit is only available until 200,000 qualified EVs have been sold in the United States by each manufacturer, at which point the credit begins to phase out for that manufacturer. In 2019, Tesla and Chevrolet are already phasing out.

Depending on where you live, you may also be eligible for EV incentives from your state, city, or utility. In the U.S., check www.energy.gov for details.

In Europe, the electrification of transportation gets from a few million to hundreds of millions of euros in subsidies in half of the Member States.

More generally, the aid given to renewables and "carbon-free" energy uses must be compared with those granted to fossil fuels. In 2015, the G20 nations gave four times more in loans and subsidies to the fossil fuel industry than to the renewable energy sector (US$71.8 billion versus US$18.7 billion). That same year, even Germany – the European leader in renewables – spent only €2 billion on incentives for green energy versus €3 billion in aid for gas, coal, and oil. If all the subsidies for diesel production in Europe or the U.S. were eliminated, the price of diesel fuel would rise 33%!

...but where will the required electricity come from?

There's nothing to worry about here! Our current distribution network is sufficient to power all the cars in the world, even if the global fleet were already converted to electricity. Indeed, the grid is scaled to supply peak power that is necessary only a few minutes a day. The rest of the time it is underutilized, so charging millions of batteries outside such peaks would not be a problem.

Explanation. Electricity demand varies from one day to the next, but has a very predictable daily cycle. Two consumption peaks are seen, one in the morning from 7 to 11, and the other at the end of the day, from 6 to 9 p.m. Demand is much lower between 9 p.m. and 7 a.m. During the nighttime trough, demand is 10-50% lower than during the peaks, and that is precisely when most private vehicles are recharged.

The mean energy consumption of an electric car is 8 to 12 kWh a day, which would amount to 5% of energy consumption if the entire U.S. fleet of cars was converted to electricity. The nocturnal and midday low points in generation would thus provide enough capacity to power all of the cars on the continent without adding a single power plant. The power companies would even rack up savings, for they

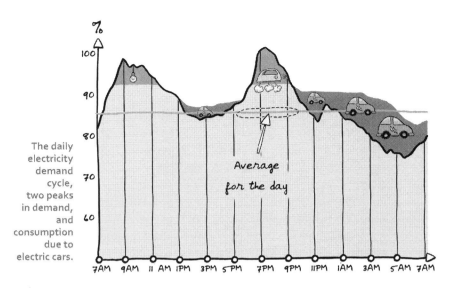

The daily electricity demand cycle, two peaks in demand, and consumption due to electric cars.

would be able to use their production plant more profitably with a steady, regular demand. The only problems that might crop up would be in the early evening during the coldest nights of the year (a limited number in most regions), during which the increase in demand due to electric vehicles could be 4% of power generation.

It is thus in the public authorities' interest to promote electric mobility, but to do so in conjunction with a rate scheme that encourages charging during off-peak hours. In this way, users would be tempted to take advantage of the lower rates and avoid charging during peak demand hours.

V2G (*Vehicle To Grid*)

Smart chargers may in the near future be able to use the storage capacities of electric cars to supply the grid with electricity. In the event of peaks in demand, the grid will draw electricity from the cars' batteries. The individual who sells her/ his car's electricity to attenuate the peak will be paid an advantageous rate. If only 5% of cars were connected to smart chargers, the power grid would double its storage capacity and eliminate all risks of winter blackouts.

This "V2G" (vehicle-to-grid) technology should be set up within the next ten years. It would be a completely logical complement to the spread of wind turbines and photovoltaic panels (intermittent energy sources). Public investment would be limited to installing "smart" electric meters.

Note. Nissan Leafs from 2018 are already V2G compatible.

...it is too slow

Ten percent of motorists are convinced that electric cars are good only for slow downtown driving "because their batteries are too small." Even though it is true that many small city compacts currently in circulation are electric, it is just as true that they are more powerful and accelerate much better than their gasoline-powered rivals. Today's electric cars are not golf carts!

The future lies with electric cars because...

...they save us time

Electric car owners are the only motorists who have filling stations in their homes. Only during non-routine long journeys do they need to stop along the way to recharge. Recharging takes much longer than filling a gas tank, but since it is done at home every night, recharging on the road is required much less often. What is more, maintenance and repairs practically disappear with an electric car: another time saving!

...they are much more awesome to drive

Why do more than 85% of electric car owners think that they will never go back to buying an ICE car? Because they prefer the smoothness, silence, and acceleration of the electric car. Then, when it comes to brand image, what could possibly be more awesome than driving without polluting like Shakira, Eva Longoria, and George Clooney?

...they are silent

The sound experience inside an electric car is very different. The sounds of the tires on the road and air brushing the body are the only things to disrupt the sound of the radio. No more changes in rpms, the revving of engines at low speed. As of 2019, U.S. and European regulations will even require makers to add an acoustic device to warn pedestrians that an electric car is approaching! However, the most surprising thing for a novice EV passenger is the lack of ignition sounds.

The Krieger, built by the electric car maker *Compagnie parisienne des voitures électriques* in 1904.
It has a range of 80 km (48 mi) and is still in working order, despite being 114 years old.

...they are robust and durable

The electric car's reduced complexity reduces the risk of breakdowns. The lack of high temperatures (no cylinder head, exhaust, or radiator), parts subject to wear (clutch), and lubricants also reduces many points of vulnerability. An electric car should thus last at least twice as long as its ICE rivals, or 300,000 rather than 150,000 mi (500,000 vs 250,000 km). The batteries, for their part, are manufacturer-guaranteed for 90,000 mi (160,000 km) or 6 years for the most timid. You can thus reasonably bank on replacing the battery twice over the car's lifetime. Nissan currently bills 2011-2015 Leaf owners $5,500 to replace the battery, plus installation. Refurbished batteries may also become the best choice when replacing a worn-out battery pack. Nissan offers reconditioned batteries for less than half the price of a brand new 24 kWh pack. And let's not forget that battery prices are falling fast.

...they are (often) cheaper to run

Compared with gasoline or diesel fuel, the cost price per mile (CPM) of a new electric car is becoming more advantageous each year, in line with the battery price trend. The scales could tip even more in the EV's favor in view of oil price-trend (a barrel of crude went from US$42 to US$74 between July 2017 and June 2018 and then to US$55 in March 2019) and new antipollution rules, for which compliance is increasingly expensive.

Pollution over Montréal.

Other favorable aspects: Low maintenance costs, lower taxes, and some preferential insurance rates (15-to-25% discounts).

...they don't smell bad

No more exhaust gases and gasoline fumes. Putting an end to emitting fine particles and nitrogen oxides and reducing carbon emissions can only improve everyone's health. The World Health Organization (WHO) has established that at least 3 million human deaths a year can be ascribed to pollution, of which 750,000 are due to the internal combustion engines used for transportation. More than 100,000 of all these deaths are caused by the nitrogen oxides emitted by diesel engines, which are a primary cause of cardiorespiratory disease.

Adopting an electric car is a small step towards solving this problem. In the medium and long run, switching to electric cars will generate huge savings for our governments by reducing the healthcare costs linked to the ill effects of pollution.

...they have the free run of city centers

More and more cities have no-go areas or congestion charges for ICE cars, the aim being to reduce noise and pollution. For example, cars entering central London must pay a congestion charge of £10 unless they are electric. Starting in 2025, a zero emissions zone in which only electric vehicles will be allowed will be instated. The ZEZ will gradually be extended to cover the entire city by 2050. If a Londoner intends to keep her/his

One of the entrances into London's congestion charging zone. Free ingress for electric vehicles, whereas the others must pay £10 ($13) and even £12.50 ($16.5) starting in 2020.

197

car more than seven years and continue to drive it in central London, buying a car that runs on petrol is already out of the question!

... they slip into traffic flows more easily

The electric car's fast, gradual acceleration makes it very easy to enter highway traffic from an on-ramp or in traffic circles. Putting in the clutch and changing gears are "20th-century passé, my dear!"

...we shall soon have no other options

Many countries and regional entities have announced the end of ICE car sales by 2040, and even earlier in some cases. More and more cities are already instituting, starting in 2019, low emissions zones from which ICE cars are banned.

Given the ten-year-or-so lifespan of today's cars, it is clear that it will be impossible to sell a second-hand ICE car starting in 2030. 2018 marked the collapse of the diesel empire; that of the gas engine will follow with a few years' lag.

... your grandchildren will thank you

Your grandchildren will be proud to tell their pals that their family was among the first to take action to leave the planet in not too bad a state.

The cult of the diesel engine

The cult of the diesel engine was for many years the main religion of European motorists. It was instituted by our governments to counter the OPEC embargoes during the oil crisis of the seventies.

The earthquake that toppled the diesel engine's throne fifty years later was of course Dieselgate, the scandal of Volkswagen's cheating about its engines' true emissions in 2015. In the past two years the public at large has effectively turned its back on diesel engines in favor of gasoline-powered, hybrid, and electric cars.

In 2040, the only way to see a piston engine could be to visit a museum.

However, under pressure from automakers, the public authorities continue to tax diesel fuel less than gasoline, which is a disguised way of subsidizing diesel fuel to the detriment of all others. Automakers are using the argument that it produces less greenhouse gas (GES) as their main lever to try to reverse the trend to abandon diesel fuel.

The European car makers' association ACEA, chaired by the big boss of Daimler-Mercedes, published a clear message for lawmakers in 2017: "No one wants electric cars! There is no charging infrastructure and it costs too much. Allow us to equip our vehicles with diesel engines and you will reduce CO_2 emissions by 20%." This figure is contested by the European Federation for Transport and Environment (T&E), which has calculated that diesel vehicles actually emit 9% more CO_2 than their gas-burning counterparts.

What is more, T & E points out that the nitrogen oxide emissions (the famous NOx) of recent diesel engines that comply with the Euro 6 standard all surpass the allowed value of 80 mg/km. This was confirmed by the German automobile

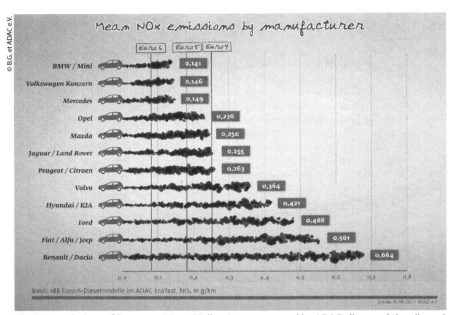

The NOx emissions of European "Euro 6" diesel cars measured by ADAC all exceed the allowed value. Some of them even fail to comply with the Euro 4 standard.

club ADAC, which tested more than 150 vehicles of the major European makes in 2017. The most polluting vehicle in the test emitted 21 times more NOx than the reference value! Under such conditions, we are entitled to doubt whether the Euro 7 engines will manage to comply with an even more stringent standard.

Predictions for 2019-2023

Predictions are hard to make, especially when they concern the future.
(Pierre Dac)

It is hard to know whether quotations found on the Internet are authentic.
(Abraham Lincoln)

Below the reader will find various announcements, predictions, and suppositions that are neither completely crazy nor completely certain. The degree of confidence that our small but impartial panel of readers gives each one is indicated by a score ranging from 1 (simple rumor) to 5 (absolute certainty).

What was known from 2018

☺ The decision was made: London cabs may be replaced by electric models only.

☺ The share of electric models in world automotive sales rose from 2% on January 1st to 3% on December 31.

☺ Electric vans, delivery trucks, and small trucks of Chinese manufacture were appearing on the European market, with SAIC's Maxus EV80 leading the pack.

☺ The demand for the Tesla Model 3 was not waning. Four-wheel-drive and "Performance" options were being added to the catalog. Production was not keeping up with demand.

☺ During the 2018 year, the share of fully electric vehicles in car sales in Norway grew 40% year-on-year to reach 31.2%. Taking plug-in vehicles into account, the EV market share reached 49.1% of the market.

☺ Tesla announced its Model Y crossover, a sort of mini-Model X, but without the "falcon wing" doors, that will be unveiled in March 2019.

☺ Fiat-Chrysler and Toyota announced the electrification of their ranges in five years' time.

2019

◌◌◌◌◌ The share of electric vehicles in Chinese sales reached 6.3% on December 31, with one million plug-in cars sold.

◌◌◌◌ The Tesla Model 3 is being released on the Chinese and European markets.

◌◌◌◌ Mini plans to put an electric Mini in its showrooms in the middle of the year. The vehicle will be based on the BMW i3 drivetrain.

◌◌◌◌ Electric cars (including plug-in hybrids) will account for 10% of sales in Europe's most advanced markets (the Netherlands, France, and Germany).

The Aston-Martin RapidE targets the high-end luxury sports car market.

◎◎◎◎ Aston Martin will start selling the RapidE, a 1,000-horse-power electric sports car with a range of 216 miles (360 km) that is based on the Rapide AMR developed with Williams Advanced Engineering. It will be built in a small series (155 cars) and should cost €200,000, with the objective being to offer a more luxurious GT (grand tourer) than the Tesla Model S.

◎◎◎◎ Tesla will manage to meet world demand for its Model 3.

◎◎◎◎ The number of Tesla Model Ys on order will exceed 200,000 by year end.

◎◎◎◎ Mercedes-Benz will launch its big SUV, the EQC, and is preparing to roll out other 100% electric vehicles under the "QC" label. U.S. availability not expected before Christmas.

◎◎◎◎ The first electric delivery trucks by Renault Trucks (a division of Geely-Volvo, as you would never guess from its name), built in Normandy, will roll onto the dealers' lots.

◎◎◎ Tesla unveils its future "cyberpunk truck" seemingly inspired by 1980s cyberpunk movie 'Blade Runner.'

Tesla will deliver its first Tesla Semi trucks to its customers.

Mazda will examine the possibility of making an electric car ("A small one, because a large car with a big battery makes no sense for Mazda," says Mr. Tanaka, R&D Manager at Mazda Europe).

Fiat-Chrysler and Toyota announce that their ranges will be electrified in about five years.

2020

140 different 100% electric models are available, to which we can add some 100 hybrids and plug-in hybrids (a Bloomberg New Energy Finance prediction). All the major automakers now have electric propulsion in their catalogs.

Tesla completes the construction of its Gigafactory 1 battery plant in Nevada.

Tesla delivers the first units of its crossover, the Model Y.

The twin makers Kia and Hyundai increase their offer of electric and plug-in hybrid cars, with 26 models in their catalog.

Several electric models are available from Porsche. The Taycan will be a sort of Panamera capable of covering 250 miles (400 km) between charges. Porsche's superchargers will be able to recharge it in 15 minutes.

Diesel vehicle sales are in free fall to the benefit of the plug-in hybrid and electric vehicle market.

Geely-Volvo puts out three new electric models plus two others under its prestigious Polestar brand.

The entire road network in both the U.S. and Europe is equipped with chargers at almost every rest stop. Lines of cars waiting to hook up to the chargers are frequent.

Tesla launches a small affordable passenger car. What will its name be? The Model Z, the Model 2?

Seat launches the Born-E, an electric car based on the MEB platform that it shares with Volkswagen's I.D. range.

Electricity grids test smart billing and V2G technology.

Government regulations require charging stations for all apartment blocks and public parking lots.

Ford launches plug-in hybrid versions of its Mustang and F-150 pickup.

Fiat-Chrysler and Toyota announce that their ranges will be electrified in five years, we promise!

2021

A spate of restructuring of car dealers; the smallest points of sale not prepared for selling electric cars shut down.

Subaru presents several electric models based on the "Global Platform" shared by many of the make's vehicles, including the well-known Impreza.

BMW starts selling its electric i4 based on the i Vision Dynamics concept car.

Tesla is worth more than US$400 billion on the stock market, which makes it Number 1 among automakers.

©Bayerische Motoren Werke

BMW iNext undergoes winter trial tests in February 2019.

One out of two new buses in Europe and North America is electric.

First major bankruptcies in the automotive industry (automakers and OEMs).

First reductions in the number of points of sale in fuel distribution networks.

Ford starts selling an SUV specifically designed for shared-vehicle fleets.

Fiat-Chrysler and Toyota announce that their ranges will be electrified in five years and it's true this time!

2022

Tipping point. Electric cars and comparable ICE cars are selling at the same prices. The price advantage of the lower cost price per mile tilts the scales in favor of fully electric cars. The S-curve of electric car adoption enters the mature phase.

Daimler now offers "electrified" versions of all its Mercedes-Benz and Smart models, which are assembled in six plants around the world. Daimler is making its own batteries in Germany, the U.S., and China from cells bought mainly from Samsung SDI.

Plug-in hybrid car sales plummet because their four-year resale value is continuing to decline.

Fiat-Chrysler and Toyota announce that their ranges will be electrified in five years at the very latest.

2025

25%. The Volkswagen group fulfills its General Manager's 2017 prediction, according to which the group wanted to become "the Number 1 in e-mobility" in 2025, albeit without giving up conventional engines. More than 30 models propelled exclusively by batteries and 50 hybrid models are sold under the group's brands: VW, Audi, Seat, Skoda,

Porsche, Bugatti, Bentley, and Lamborghini. Volkswagen is banking on a 25% market share for electric propulsion, or 2-3 million vehicles a year.

Infinity, Nissan's luxury arm, is selling 25% of its models in "pure electric" versions and 25% as plug-in hybrids.

The Renault Trezor concept car – car of the future?

Daimler-Benz (Mercedes) has an EQ range of ten vehicles based on a platform designed specifically for electric propulsion. Production is boosted by the recently opened lithium-ion battery plant, which cost more than $500 million.

16%. Electric mobility accounts for 16% of the world market according to the bank BNP Paribas and Union of Swiss Banks' (UBS) analysts.

3.4%. Electric mobility accounts for 3.4% of the world market according to the consultancy IHS Markit.

The PSA group (Peugeot-Citroën-Opel-Vauxhall) proposes electric or hybrid versions of all its vehicle ranges, for more than 40 "electrified" models.

Fiat-Chrysler and Toyota announce that their ranges will be electrified within five years; it's been decided!

2030

All the major automakers have added autonomous cars to their catalogs. The first cars without steering wheels and pedals appear on the roads.

Volkswagen completes its $40 billion electric mobility investment plan and proposes more than 300 models propelled by electric motors or hybrid systems.

According to Honda's predictions, 50% of its total vehicle output consists of full-electric and fuel-cell vehicles.

To wrap up

2019 will be a key year in the history of electric cars. While the "point of no return" in the S-curve of this new technology's take-up will not be achieved, it is in sight, and all the indicators point to its' being reached very soon, in at most three years.

The multiple announcements of the intentions of all the major automakers, steady decline in battery prices, public authorities' statements in favor of electric mobility, and above all the banning of ICE cars in a growing number of major cities, such as Los Angeles, London, Barcelona, Milan, Vancouver, and many more, by 2030 are indicators that will not lead us astray. Whole countries have even declared themselves ready to ban fossil fuel-burning engines in the near future: India, Israël, and Denmark (in 2030), Norway (in 2035), France and the United Kingdom (in 2040), and Canada and China (in 2040?). As for motorists, a growing number are seriously considering replacing their current cars with plug-in or electric cars before 2023.

Up until 2017, the most likely scenario was that struggles for influence would take place between electric vehicles and increasingly economical and less polluting ICE cars. However, since the total ban on internal combustion engines is no longer a possibility, but now a certainty, the players in place have engaged in a struggle for market share once again. The watchful observer will have noticed that the major automakers are no longer fighting electric cars openly. Rather, they are tending to focus more on showing how much they are pioneering in the field.

Tesla, as the world's only manufacturer of solely electric cars, is playing a leading role in electric mobility more and more. It is now going to have to take on the majority of automakers, who will have to become serious competitors on pain of disappearing. What will Tesla's position on the automotive market be a few years from now? Will it take the role of the outsider that has made a place for itself in the sun or that of a small manufacture that continues to play a marginal role? The growth of Tesla's production lines in the last two years was astonishing but developments in 2019 and 2020 will probably be the deciding factor.

Will driverless cars revolutionize the entire automotive sector even before the revolution of transportation's electrification comes to an end? It is still a little too early to say but, here, too, the question asked more and more often is "when?" rather than "what if?"

Make no mistake about it: Whether we want it or not, the electric revolution is under way. It will change all of our lives in the next few years.

Glossary

12 VOLTS. 12 volts is the voltage used for all accessories in a car. This voltage is low enough to avoid all risks of electrocution. The negative terminal is connected to the chassis. To power an accessory, a single wire suffices, as the return current flows through the chassis.

48 VOLTS. 48 volts is the highest voltage that can be used without the risk of electrocution. As the connections require cables that are four times as thick as for 12 volts, it is possible to run more powerful accessories, such as air conditioners, the starter-alternator used for stop and start systems, and energy recovery in non-rechargeable hybrids.

AC (ALTERNATING CURRENT). The electric current in the public grid is always alternating. It goes through 60 positive alternations and 60 negative alternations a second. Its frequency is thus 60 hertz (50 Hz in Europe). The advantage of AC is that it is easy to change its voltage using a transformer. It thus is easier to go from a high-voltage line (for long-distance transmission) to lower voltage for local use.

AEB (AUTOMATIC EMERGENCY BRAKING). A feature that alerts a driver to an imminent crash and helps him use the maximum braking capacity of the car.

AMPERE. Unit of intensity of an electric current. The higher the amperage, the thicker the transmission wire must be to avoid overheating. The maximum current in a standard electrical 204V outlet is 16 A. The corresponding copper wires must be 2.5 mm² in cross-section.

ASYNCHRONOUS MOTOR. *See* **Induction Motor**

AVAS (Acoustic Vehicle Alerting System). An acoustic warning device that simulates ICE engine noise from ignition until about 12 mph (20 km/h). The driver can deactivate it.

Battery. The battery, which is the electric car's energy source, is composed of a few modules or subsets that are easier to handle. Each module is itself composed of a few dozen (for the rectangular formats) or hundred (for the cylindrical formats) cells. The maximum voltage of a battery ranges from 300 to 800 V, depending on the model.

BEV (Battery Electric Vehicle). The abbreviation commonly used to refer to 100% electric cars.

BMS (Battery Management System). The BMS balances the charges of all the cells in a lithium-ion battery. At the end of charging it discharges the most highly-charged cells slightly and tops up the charges of the less-charged cells until the voltage of all the cells is identical.

Brick. A battery that is completely discharged to the point where it is impossible to recharge it normally. This happens if a battery discharged to 0% is left unconnected for a long time. Self-discharging then makes it impossible for the control electronics to work normally and can even damage the battery cells. Except in extreme cases, the manufacturer may be able to reactivate charging, but permanent damage to the battery is possible. The manufacturer's warranty usually does not cover this risk.

C max (maximum charging rate). The maximum charging rate gives the speed at which a battery can be recharged. If C = 1, the battery can be charged from 0 to 100% in 1 hour. If C = 0.5, this will take 2 hours and if C = 2, a half-hour will suffice.

Capacity (in kWh). The rated capacity of a battery is the amount of energy that it can contain. It is expressed in kilowatt-hours. To avoid overcharging or draining a battery completely, the usable capacity is often used. This is the capacity available between the voltage limits set by the manufacturer so as not to damage the cells (typically 2.9 to 4.2 V).

CARB (California Air Resources Board). California's primary state agency in charge of protecting public health from air pollution. Its regulations promoted the development of hybrid and electric vehicles.

Car sharing. Service offered by people or companies to put vehicles at the disposal of a client network. Uber, Lyft, and BlaBlaCar are examples of major car-sharing groups. The car-sharing companies that own their vehicles have been the first to take an interest in autonomous cars.

CCS (Combined Charging System). Also called Combo. A fast-charging socket standard that belongs to the Type 2 category and is governed by the international standard IEC 62196. Many fast-charging stations in Europe are compatible with it. In the future, charging at up to 350 kW will be possible on a CCS socket. Germany already requires that there be at least one CCS connection in all public charging places and this requirement is spreading fast in Europe and around the world.

CELL. The cell is the basic element of a rechargeable lithium-ion battery. Its voltage ranges from 2.9 to 4.2 V, with the reference rated value usually being 3.7 V. There are several chemical and mechanical variations (NCM, NCA, and LFP for the former; rectangular and cylindrical for the latter). It must not be mistaken for a lithium battery, which is not rechargeable.

CHARGING. Process that restores electricity to a battery. The source is an AC (single- or three-phase) or DC socket. The energy is converted to a voltage and amperage that are optimized by an onboard electronic circuit that optimizes the charging speed without harming battery life.

CHARGING INFRASTRUCTURE. All of the charging points in public and privately-owned places, including the parking lots of apartment buildings and shopping malls. The growth of the electric car market depends greatly on the charging infrastructure's expansion, to the point where the public authorities have a major role to play.

CHARGING STATION. There are two types: the simple wall box and the fast-charging station, also called a supercharger. In both cases, the cable is powered only when it is connected to the vehicle and its insulated status has been checked. Wall box connection uses single-phase 220 V AC (power of up to 7 kW) or three-phase 400 V AC (power up to 22 kW). Superchargers supply DC at between 200 and 450 V (power ranging from 50 to 150 kW).

CHADEMO. The Japanese fast-charging socket standard, whereby up to 62.5 kW of power is delivered by DC. Many fast-charging stations in Europe are compatible with the ChaDeMo standard.

CO_2 (CARBON DIOXIDE). Carbon dioxide is a greenhouse gas. Burning one gallon (about 6.3 pounds) of fuel produces some 20 lb (9.6 Kg) of CO_2. Pursuant to U.S. EPA standards, the mean CO_2 emissions of vehicles sold by an automaker will be limited to 250 g CO_2 per mile. In Europe, the limit is set to 152 g/mi (95 g/km) in 2021 and as low as 106 g/mi (66 g/km) in 2030. This statutory requirement explains the arrival of electric and hybrid vehicles on our roads, which may or may not be accompanied by the desire to sell them *en masse*.

CRUISE CONTROL. A system that keeps a vehicle running at a constant speed automatically, regardless of the grade or type of terrain.

Adaptive cruise control can also reduce the speed of a vehicle that follows a slower vehicle. It keeps a safety distance between the two vehicles. This type of automatic response is classified as "Autonomous Driving Level 2."

CUV (Crossover Utility Vehicle). The crossover is a car that has inherited the features of the sedan and Sport Utility Vehicle (SUV). While it has better fuel economy and is less expensive than the big SUVs, the crossover conserves the latter's high hip-point seating and roomy interior.

DC (Direct Current). Direct current never changes polarity. It is thus the current that enters and exits batteries. It is easy to turn alternating current into direct current using a rectifier. The reverse is more complicated and requires the use of an electronic circuit called an inverter.

Decarbonization. All of the measures taken to reduce an activity's carbon emissions in general, and CO_2 emissions in particular. The aim of decarbonization is to mitigate anthropogenic (meaning "caused by humans") global warming. Decarbonizing transportation entails powering vehicles with electricity that is generated without using fossil fuels.

Diesel. Type of engine invented by Rudolf Diesel and thus, by extension, the name given in certain countries to the fuel that it uses.

It is also called diesel oil or gasoil in some countries, but "road diesel" and "gas oil" are used for different purposes in the English-speaking world. It is a light fuel obtained by refining oil. Due to the harmful health effects of the fine particles and nitrogen oxides that its combustion generates, road diesel is taxed heavily in Switzerland and Denmark. It is more expensive than gas in the U.S., but cheaper in Europe because of lower excise taxes on diesel than on gasoline. This difference has narrowed over the years and should even disappear by 2021.

Dieselgate. An industrial and health scandal caused by the Volkswagen group using fraudulent techniques in all its makes to reduce the apparent emissions of the pollutants nitrogen oxides and CO_2 from their diesel engines during approval testing but letting these emissions go well beyond the legal standards during normal use. Dieselgate affected more than 11 million vehicles between 2009 and 2015 and cost VW more than US$ 30 billion. This amount included US$2 billion in compensation demanded by the U.S. authorities to finance Electrify America, a U.S.-wide charging infrastructure program for electric cars.

Drivetrain. The series of electrical and mechanical elements stretching from the car's energy reserve to its wheels. There are two main types: thermal and electrical. Thermal drivetrain: fuel tank, internal combustion engine, clutch, gearbox, differential, and wheels. Electric drivetrain: battery, electronics module, motor, step-down transformer, differential, and wheels. The electric car's drivetrain (or powertrain) is much simpler, comprising a score of moving parts as opposed to a thousand in an ICE car.

ELECTRIFICATION. The term used by automakers to have the public think that they are really motivated to sell electric vehicles. It consists of adding something electric to the vehicle. An "electrified" car can be a hybrid, whether or not plug-in, or an electric car. The sentence "Our models will be electrified" means "We shall have at least a hybrid version of each of our models," but definitely not "All our models will be electric only."

ELECTRODE. Element of an electrical conductor that releases or captures electrons. The two electrodes of a lithium-ion cell are the anode (negative electrode) and cathode (positive electrode).

EMISSIONS. Carbon dioxide (CO_2), nitrogen oxide (NOx), and fine-particle emissions are forms of air pollution. *See also* **Zero emission**.

ENERGY EFFICIENCY. Ratio between the incoming and outgoing energy of a procedure, such as the charging-discharging of a battery or operation of a motor or engine.

The energy efficiency of gasoline from "well to wheels" (W2W), *i.e.*, from the oil well to the wheels of an ICE car, is on the order of 14%. That of electricity from home photovoltaic panels to the electric car's wheels can exceed 85%.

EPA. The EPA cycle is used in the U.S. like the WLTP in Europe to compare vehicle fuel economy. The EPA cycle is in two parts: city and highway operation. The EPA test gives results that are close to reality under good weather conditions. *See also* **NEDC** and **WLTP**.

E-PEDAL. *See* **One-pedal Drive.**

EURO 6. The Euro 6 standard imposes an 80 mg/km nitrogen oxide emissions (NOx) cutoff on cars with diesel engines. In practice, not a single diesel engine meets this standard at all operating speeds. The standard also limits fine-particle emissions, which obliges manufacturers to fit their vehicles with special filters.

EV (ELECTRIC VEHICLE). Acronym used to refer to electric cars and trucks.

EVSE (ELECTRIC VEHICLE SUPPLY EQUIPMENT). Equipment needed to charge an electric vehicle at home. *See* **Wall box.**

FAST CHARGING. Charging that can restore a battery's charge from less than 10% to 80% in an hour at most. This requires a fast-charging station or "supercharger."

The charging is actually fast only up to about the 80% charge level, then it slows down to avoid over-charging certain cells (there are always tiny disparities between the cells in a battery). The charging speed for this last fraction depends on how sophisticated the BMS connected to the battery is.

FCEV (FUEL CELL ELECTRIC VEHICLE). Also called "hydrogen vehicle". The term "FCEV" is often used in opposition to BEV for battery electric vehicle. An FCEV emits no pollutants locally; it discharges only water and heat.

FUEL CELL. System for transforming hydrogen into electricity by a chemical reaction. Also called "fuel stack" because of the large number of identical elements stacked end to end. The energy yield of a fuel cell is about 50%, with the rest lost as heat.

FUEL CONSUMPTION. The fuel consumption of an ICE car is expressed in miles per gallon (mpg) in North America and Great Britain and in liters/100 km in Europe. That of an electric car is expressed in kilo-watt-hours per miles or kilometer per kWh (mi/kWh and kWh/km, respectively). Direct comparison of the two is possible only if the prices of the fuel in question and kWh of electricity are known. The fuel consumption of different vehicles is compared by running a standard test cycle (EPA, NEDC, or WLTC).

G20. Group of Twenty. An international forum of nineteen countries plus the European Union set up to promote the discussion of global economic issues and international financial stability.

GASOLINE (OR GAS). A fuel produced by refining oil. Gasoline is sold at highly variable prices depending on the country and tax regimen. For example, it costs US\$1.00 per liter on average in the world but only US\$0.35/l in Koweit and US\$2.08/l in Iceland. Its average price in the U.S. is about US\$0.83/l (Official data, Aug. 31, 2018). In Europe, gasoline is referred as petrol.

GHG (GREENHOUSE GAS). Greenhouse gases are gases that absorb the infrared rays emitted by the Earth and thus counter the natural cooling of the Earth's atmosphere. The main GHGs are water vapor, carbon dioxide (CO_2), methane (CH_4), nitrous oxide (N_2O), and ozone (O_3). The GHG with the greatest effect is water vapor (72% of the total effect). Three-quarters of the CO_2 in the air comes from human activities.

GIGAWATT (GW). One billion watts (a unit of power). *See also* **Megawatt** and **Kilowatt**.

GIGAWATT HOUR (GWH). One billion watt-hours or one million kilowatt-hours (kWh) (a unit of energy).

HEAT ENGINE. (aka **ICE**). The heat engine converts heat (or chemical energy) into mechanical energy. It is broken down into two categories – the internal and external combustion engine. Hence the term is often used to refer to internal combustion engines powered by gasoline, diesel, natural gas (methane), or LPG (liquefied petroleum gas, which is a mixture of propane and methane). Whatever the fuel used, an ICE always gives off CO_2. "Heat engine" and "thermal engine" are synonymous. *See also* **ICE**.

HOV (HIGH-OCCUPANCY VEHICLE LANE). Also known as a carpool lane, an HOV is a traffic lane reserved for the exclusive use of vehicles with a driver and one or more passengers.

HP. Abbreviation for "horsepower," a widely used unit of power that equals 375 watts (0.375 kW) in the metric system. To convert back, 1 kW = 1.36 hp.

HYBRID. A hybrid vehicle combines two energy sources, typically an internal combustion engine and an electric motor powered by a battery that is recharged by energy recovery. In a non-rechargeable hybrid vehicle, all the energy comes from the fuel.

HYDROGEN. Hydrogen is a very light gas and the most abundant element in the universe. It can be stored as a liquid, which requires very low temperatures, or as a gas, which requires very high pressure, only. It is produced by reforming the hydrogen in fossil fuels. It can also be extracted from water by electrolysis, but current procedures have low yields and are very expensive (they use platinum).

ICE (INTERNAL COMBUSTION ENGINE) As its name indicates, an ICE burns fuel internally. The energy that is released is turned into mechanical energy by a complex set of components: compressor, injector, cylinders, pistons, crankshaft, valves, exhaust system, and so on. The most common fuels are petrol, diesel, liquefied petroleum gas (LPG), and natural gas (methane). These engines' yields range from 25 to 42%, calculated by the difference between the latent energy contained in the fuel and the energy of rotation on the drive shaft. The rest of the energy is dissipated as heat.

IEA (INTERNATIONAL ENERGY AGENCY). The IEA's aim is to develop clean, reliable, cheap energy for its twenty-nine Member States. Internet site: iea.org.

IEC 62196. International standard for charging connectors. *See* **Type 2** and **CCS**.

IGBT (INSULATED GATE BIPOLAR TRANSISTOR). An IGBT is a large transistor capable of connecting or disconnecting very high electrical currents at the command of a low-power signal, such as a computer's. The invention of the IGBT made it possible to control countless electrical appliances, from power drill motors to electric truck motors, via computers.

INDUCTIVE CHARGING. The idea of charging one's battery without having to plug it into the grid is appealing. In reality, i inductive coupling is more difficult: The car must be positioned very precisely over the charger's induction loop and the yield of the contactless connection does not exceed 90%. Currently, the additional cost of the inductive charger, added to an electricity bill that is rising by 10%, does not plead in favor of rushing to adopt this solution.

INDUCTION MOTOR. The induction motor needs an electronic module to propel a car. However, it has the advantage of not depending on expensive materials such as neodyme, like the permanent-magnet motor. The induction motor is 20% heavier, but has a better yield running at intermediate speed and tolerates bursts of power well. It is thus better suited to large sedans than to small city models. It is also called an asynchronous motor.

KILOWATT (KW). One thousand watts (a unit of power). Power is an amount of energy per time unit. A kilowatt is equal to 1.36 hp.

KILOWATT HOUR (KWH). One million watt-hours (a unit of energy), *i.e.*, the energy of 1 kW during one hour. The official unit of energy in the metric system is the joule (J). However, this unit is much too small to be used in everyday conversation in this context (1 kWh = 3.6 MJ). A kWh costs 12 cents in the United States and 12 Canadian cents in Canada. The mean price of a kWh in Europe is €0.20.

LIDAR (LIGHT DETECTION AND RANGING). A kind of radar that operates with a laser beam that detects the distances of objects within its range. All autonomous vehicles (except Teslas) use LIDARs to give their electronic brains precise pictures of the surrounding world. A modern LIDAR has a range of 100 m and is accurate to 2 cm at this distance. One thing is for sure regarding LIDARs: They are very expensive.

LIFE OR LIFESPAN. The life of a lithium-ion battery is expressed in number of cycles. According to the manufacturers, it ranges from 600 to 6,000 cycles, but depends above all on the way a charging-discharging cycle is defined. The electronics of an electric car is calibrated to avoid overcharging and prevent excessive discharging. Consequently, a battery can withstand several thousand cycles. To express battery life in miles, you have to multiply the number of cycles by the distance covered on a fully-charged battery. That explains why the manufacturers have no qualms about guaranteeing their batteries for 6-8 years and many thousands of miles.

LITHIUM. The lightest metal on Earth. It oxidizes very quickly. It is plentiful in seawater but its preferred industrial extraction is from salt flats, where it is concentrated in the form of salts. Its price has skyrocketed because of rising demand but should stabilize in the near future when new deposits begin to be worked.

LITHIUM-ION. One of the most effective electrochemical methods for storing electricity.

MEGAWATT(MW). One million watts (a unit of power unit). *See also* **Kilowatt**.

MEGAWATT-HOUR (MWH). One million watt-hours (a unit of energy), or 1,000 kWh.

MENNEKES. A type of charging socket, synonymous with Type 2.

MSRP. Also called or sticker price, MSRP is the car manufacturer's suggested retail price. The exact selling price is negociated with the dealer.

NEDC (NEW EUROPEAN DRIVING CYCLE). Theoretical standard test course used to compare vehicles' ranges, fuel consumption, and pollutant emissions. The vehicle accelerates and decelerates, mainly between 0 and 50 km/h, for twenty minutes, with a single burst of speed above 100 km/h lasting a few seconds. The consumption and pollution levels recorded by this test method actually underestimates real performance by at least 20%, and sometimes as much as 50%. Now in 2019 the NEDC is mandatorily being replaced by the more stringent WLTP.

NEV (NEW ENERGY VEHICLE). This term, which is used primarily in China, includes the PHEV, BEV, and FCV.

NHTSA (NATIONAL HIGHWAY TRAFFIC SAFETY ADMINISTRATION). U.S. administration in charge of highway traffic safety.

NICKEL. A shiny, oxidation-resistant, conducting metal used in metal coins, guitar strings, and electrical connections, especially in batteries. It is fairly cheap and easy to recycle. More than 50% of the nickel used in the world is recycled.

NOx. Abbreviation encompassing the various nitrogen oxides (NO, NO_2, N_2O, N_2O_3, etc.). These regulated air pollutants are the main cause of acid rain and contribute to the development of algal blooms. NO_2 is also a greenhouse gas. All these gases irritate the bronchi and reduce the blood's oxygenating power. Young children and asthmatics are particularly sensitive to their effects. Nitrogen oxides also lower resistance to germs.

NTSB (NATIONAL TRANSPORTATION SAFETY BOARD). U.S. body in charge of road safety.

ONE-PEDAL DRIVE. This consists of controlling an electric vehicle's speed with the accelerator pedal alone: pushing down on it to go faster, releasing it to go slower and even to come to a complete halt. Nissan calls this method the "e-pedal." Most electric vehicles include a way of regulating the force of deceleration. This driving method enhances the car's range, as decelerating recovers energy and thus recharges the battery. The brake pedal is used only for emergency braking and to choose the stopping position very precisely.

OVERLOAD. Overloading a lithium-ion cell beyond its allowed maximum voltage (typically 4.1 or 4.2 V) can damage it beyond repair. That is why the electronic charging circuit is always part of the vehicle and calibrated to manage the battery with which it is paired optimally.

PARALLEL HYBRID. In this type of vehicle, the ICE and electric motor can both contribute to propulsion, with the electric motor used at low speeds and to boost accelerations. The ICE can also transfer energy to the battery, if necessary, by using the electric motor as a generator. Regenerative braking is also possible. All non-rechargeable hybrid cars are parallel hybrids.

PERMANENT-MAGNET MOTOR. In a permanent-magnet motor, the rotor consists of a permanent magnet encased in a steel block. It is very light and compact and has a better yield than an induction motor, although its yield declines slightly at high speed. It tolerates high peaks of power less well than induction motors.

PHEV (PLUG-IN HYBRID ELECTRIC VEHICLE). Unlike the hybrid car, the plug-in hybrid's battery can be recharged by plugging it into a source of electricity, just like an electric car. Depending on the size of its battery, it can behave like an electric car over a variable (but usually fairly short) distance.

POWER (RATED, PEAK). Power is an amount of energy per unit time. Power thus corresponds to an energy flux. It is expressed in watts (W) or multiples thereof. In cars, horsepower (hp) and kilowatt (kW) are commonly used. A kilowatt is equal to 1.36 hp. The rated power of an engine or motor is the power it can deliver indefinitely. Its peak power is the maximum power that it can provide for a short period of time (typically 10 seconds).

POWER ELECTRONICS. Most electronic circuits process information in the form of very low-power signals, as occurs in a computer or telephone. Certain electronic components, called "power electronics," are switches that can connect and disconnect very large currents, such as those of motors and batteries. These circuits are fairly bulky and give off heat. They must thus be cooled by air or a liquid. *See also* **IGBT**.

POWERTRAIN. *See* **Drivetrain**.

RADAR (RADIO DETECTION AND RANGING). System for detecting objects by measuring the time traveled by a radio wave that is reflected by an object within its range. RADAR is effective for determining the distance of even a distant object easily but is not very useful to determine exact shape or contours. Do not mix up RADAR and the short-range ultrasound sensors that are used to detect how close one is to a nearby obstacle.

RANGE. Distance that a car can cover on a full charge or tank of fuel. An ICE car has a range of from 180 to 420 mi (300 to 700 km) or even more. Today's electric cars have ranges of from 90 to 300 mi (150 to 500 km). In 2020 these values should be around 150 to 360 mi (250 to 600 km). In very cold weather the range can drop 15-30% below the manufacturer's stated values.

RARE EARTHS. Group of metals that are rather widespread (giving the lie to their name) but not always very easy to extract from the ground. They are used to make lasers, as additives in diesel fuel, and in catalytic converters. The rare earths include neodyme, a metal used in permanent-magnet motors. The main rare earth mines are found in Australia, France, and especially China.

REFORMING. Method for producing hydrogen from a natural gas, particularly methane. Steam methane reforming (SMR) generates a mixture of hydrogen and CO (carbon monoxide). The latter is then removed in the form of CO_2. The energy yield of SMR is on the order of 80%.

REGENERATIVE BRAKING. Regenerative braking recovers the vehicle's kinetic energy by using the motor as a generator. The generated current is re-injected into the battery. If you slam on the brakes, the regenerative effect may be insufficient – it is limited by the motor's maximum power – and you will have to use the conventional mechanical brakes. Regenerative braking is the only way to recharge the battery of a non-rechargeable hybrid car. Its advantages include less wear on the mechanical brakes and thus a low level of dust-particle release as well as reduced maintenance costs.

RESIDUAL/REMAINING RANGE. "Residual range" is used to refer to the distance that can be covered at a given point in time. Example: If a car has a range of 250 mi and a 50% charge, the residual range is 125 mi.

RETHINKX. A group of futurists that includes Tony Seba, the author of "Rethinking Transportation", a reference document for TaaS.

REX (RANGE EXTENDER). Name given to the small heat engine in the plug-in BMW i3 series hybrid. The American automaker Workhorse also uses BMW REXes in its W-15 pickup and E-Gen and N-Gen vans.

SELF-DISCHARGE. Characteristic of a lithium-ion battery that discharges slowly at rest. This type of battery must be recharged periodically (typically once a month) to avoid draining it completely, which would be detrimental to battery life. Self-discharge varies with the chemistry used. It is higher in the lithium-polymer (LFP) batteries used by BYD.

SERIES HYBRID. In this type of vehicle, propulsion comes from the electric motor only. The ICE is connected to a generator that recharges the battery but does not drive the wheels. Series hybrids are always plug-in hybrids (PHEV). Typical examples are the BMW i3 REX and Chevrolet Volt.

SINGLE-PHASE CURRENT. Alternating current carried by two strands of wire. The normal voltage of single-phase current in the world is 220V, except in North America, Japan, and Saudi Arabia, where it is 110V but actually fluctuates between 100 and 127V. The 110V power supply handicaps the charging speed of an electric vehicle considerably.

SMARTPHONE. Just for information, the "smart mobile phone" is known by a variety of names in the French-speaking world: "portable" in France, "cellulaire" or "téléphone intelligent" in Québec, "GSM" in Belgium, "natel" in Switzerland, etc.

SOC (STATE OF CHARGE). A battery's state of charge is displayed as a percentage of the total amount available. A given value does not always correspond to the same range (in miles), because the range also depends on temperature.

SPECIFIC ENERGY. Amount of energy per unit of mass. It is expressed in watt-hours per kg (Wh/kg) or kilowatt-hours per kg (kWh/kg). A 500 kg (1,100 lb), 90 kWh Tesla Model S battery has a specific energy of 160 Wh/kg. The constant progress being made in the field gives us reason to expect specific energy levels of 260 Wh/kg in 2020. Be careful not to compare the specific energies of lithium-ion cells alone with those of complete batteries, which include other elements such as the housing, coolant, BMS, etc.

START-STOP SYSTEM. A system that shuts down an ICE automatically as soon as the vehicle stops and starts it up again when the brake is released. The vehicle must be equipped with a reinforced starter, as is the case in many hybrid cars. The Stop & Start technology gives the car a more "environmentally friendly" image, but actually improves fuel economy by a tiny fraction (except in the official NEDC test). In contrast, it increases mechanical wear, which can increase maintenance costs.

STARTUP. An innovative young company that is developing and marketing a new idea, concept, product, or service.

STATIONARY BATTERY. A battery used to store electricity for stationary use. More and more batteries are used by home owners who generate photovoltaic electricity or want to free themselves from the grid.

SUV (SPORT UTILITY VEHICLE). This is a three- or five-door high-riding recreational vehicle that can cope with off-road terrain but is never driven off-road. It is increasingly popular in North America and Europe and is used to pull trailers or, even more often, to drive the kids to school. The Tesla Model X is an electric SUV. (*Note*: The abbreviation VUS may also be seen in French-speaking Quebec.)

TaaS (TRANSPORT AS A SERVICE). An economic model of mobility that is based on the pooling of means of transport, spread of autonomous taxis, and carsharing. The massive adoption of TaaS would not necessarily reduce the number of miles driven or pollution stemming from transportation. It would, however, greatly reduce the number of cars on the road, thereby improving general mobility and freeing up space in towns and cities.

THREE-PHASE CURRENT. A set of three alternating currents that are synchronized but with staggered cycles. The normal voltages of three-phase current are 400 V between two phases and 220 V between each phase and the ground. The three-phase current has several advantages over single-phase current, such as being able to carry high power more easily and having less power loss over long-distance transmission lines.

TYPE 2. A very widespread charging socket, also known as a Mennekes socket after the name of its original manufacturer. The Type 2 socket delivers from 3 to 43.5 kW, and even up to 120 kW in the future. It is the official charging standard chosen by the European Commission (Standard IEC 62196). In Europe, Teslas use the standardized Type 2 socket, but also use it for DC charging on superchargers.

ULEZ (ULTRA LOW EMISSION ZONE). A zone set up in London where polluting vehicles will have to pay a tax starting in April 2019. Petrol-burning cars will have to comply with the Euro 4 standard and diesel cars will have to meet the Euro 6 standard to escape paying this tax.

UMC (UNIVERSAL MOBILE CONNECTOR). The mobile charging cable or charger is the electronic system that injects the alternating or direct current with which it is supplied into the battery. That entails regulating the voltage and intensity of the current while monitoring the battery's temperature and charge level. The charger is always an integral part of the vehicle. It is sometimes called a "universal mobile connector" or UMC. The cable-external housing unit that connects a home electric socket to the car is not a charger, but a safety device that limits the intensity of the current being used and checks that the connection is secure.

VOLT. The SI unit of electromotive force; the difference in electric potential between two points of a conducting wire when an electric current of one ampere dissipates one watt of power between those points. One also speaks of "voltage."

W2W (Well to Wheels). *See* **Energy efficiency**.

Wall box. A wall-mounted box with a connector for charging electric cars. The registered name "Wallbox®" is interchangeable with the common name for this type of electric vehicle supply equipment (EVSE). A wall box contains safety devices, a circuit breaker, and an optional means of identifying the user for subsequent billing (a badge or card reader). The power of a wall box can vary from 3 to 30 kW.

Watt. Unit of power.

WLTC (Worldwide Light vehicles Test Cycle). European automakers were supposed to use a new cycle that is more representative of real driving conditions than the NEDC test, namely, the WLTC, starting in 2018. However, as an adaptation period was foreseen until September 2018, they have been delaying as much as they can, because the figures will obviously be less to their advantage. The WLTC values are still often converted to "NEDC equivalent values" during a transition period that may extend to 2020 for certain countries, with each country deciding the date on which it will base its vehicle taxes on the WLTC rather than the NEDC.

ZEV (zero emission vehicle). A vehicle that emits no pollutants.

ZEV Credits. A California regulation requiring vehicle manufacturers to bring to and operate in California a certain percent of ZEVs or vehicles with near-zero tailpipe emissions. If not, they can buy "ZEV credits" from manufacturers producing ZEVs over the required threshold.

The electric car on the Web

The main references are assembled and above all updated on this book's web page (see below). There you will find a host of links to the reference documents mentioned in the text as well as other useful information, such as supplier websites, explanatory videos, market analyses, a list of clubs and associations, and so on.

www.theelectriccar.xyz

Acknowledgments

I should like to thank the many collaborators and contributors who made this volume what it is, while apologizing for not naming them all. Special thanks go to all those who provided statistics, quotes, and illustrations: Alissa André, Sales Manager of *Simon André véhicules électriques*, Canada; Christiane Baumann-Lages of Phœnix Contact, Germany; Byron Carrier of Earthly Religion, USA; Steven Colla, business development manager at Allego, Belgium; Scott Crowder, Corporate Communications Manager at Metroline, UK; Josephine Dusol of Plugsurfing GmbH, Germany; Dr. Maarten Messagie of Brussels Free University (VUB), Belgium; Leatitia Nussbaumer, Support Manager at ChargeMap, France; Erwin Raets of EVChargeKing, Belgium; Jack Rickard, founder of EVTV Motor Verks, USA; Michael Sivak of Michigan's Transport Research Institute; and Joris Steenman, Communications Coordinator at Tesla Belgique.

The drawings and diagrams are the work of Benjamin Golinvaux. Nor can I forget the publishing house NowFuture, without which you would not have a copy of this book in your hands!

Thanks also go to the press offices of the companies that gave us information and authorized us to publish photographs of their products: ADAC, Allego, Audi, Aston Martin, BAIC, BMW, BYD, Charging Plaza, Chevrolet, Citroën, Daimler-Mitsubishi, Deutsche Post, Eco-Motion, Ford Motor Company, Geely, General Motors, Honda, Hyundai, Kia, Lyft, Peugeot, Mahindra, Mennekes, Navya, NHTSA, Nio, Nikola, Nissan, Northvolt, Nuro, Opel, Peugeot, Phœnix contact, Polestar, Renault, Robomart, Saab, Subaru, Tesla, TheElectricTaxi, Toyota, Uber, Udelv, Volkswagen, Volvo, Voltacharging, Waymo, Williams Advanced Engineering, Workhorse, and Zytek Automotive.

Among the countless sources of information that modern technology now makes available, let me acknowledge the following in particular: Acti-VE, AMPERes, AddEnergie Technologies, Automobile Club of Southern California, *Automobile Propre*, Auto Notebook, *Auto Verte*, Autoexpress, Avere-France, AVEM, AvéQ, Battery University, Bloomberg New Energy Finance, BMWi3 Blogspot, *Boîtier Rouge*, *Branchez-vous Québec*, Breaking Energy, Breezcar, Byton, CCFA, Centre for Alternative Technology, Charged Electric Vehicle Magazine, ChargeHub, Clean Technica, Climate Action Network, CREG (Belgium's electricity and gas regulatory commission), Desmog Blog, Ecotricity, EENews, Eiver-car, Electrek, Electric Car Trends, Electric Car Reports, Electric Vehicle Wiki, Electrify America, Enovos, Environmental Defense Fund, Euractiv, European Alternative Fuel Observatory, European Commission (D.G. for Energy, DG for Climate Action and DG Mobility), Evannex, EV Driven, EV News, Evobsession, EV-Volumes, FreewireTech, Gas2, Gateway Electric Vehicle Club, Go Ultra Low, Green Angel Syndicate, Green Car Reports, Greentech Media, Green Technology, Green Transportation, Hybrid Cars, IEEE Spectrum, Ionity, InsideEVs, Institute for Local Self-Reliance, Interesting Engineering, International Energy Agency, *Le Circuit Électrique*, *Les Numériques*, Maarten Steinbuch, MIT Technology Review, *Moteur Nature*, Motor Legend, Natural Resources Canada (rncan.gc.ca), NewCo Shift, New Motion, Ourworldindata.org, Plugin Cars,

Protégez-vous, PV Europe, Queen's University, ReNew Australia, RethinkX, *Roulez électrique Québec*, Sigma-Tec, SF Motors, SpeakEV, Sustainable Enterprises Media, TeslaMondo, Tony Seba, Teslanomics, Tesla Motors Club, Teslarati, The City Fix, The Conversation, The Foundation for the Economics of Sustainability, The International Council on Clean Transportation, The Tesla Show, Transport & Environment, Transport Evolved, Treehugger, Union of Concerned Scientists, *Université catholique de Louvain*, University of Canterbury, University of Tennessee at Chattanooga, *Un point cinq*, UQM Technologies, Visual Capitalist, Voitureelectrique.net, WattEv2Buy, Wikipedia, Wired, Zap-Map, Ze-Mo, Zev Alliance, and Zotye Auto. Continue the excellent work you do disseminating information!

Finally, I should like to thank the group of readers who hunted down syntax errors, grammar mistakes, typos, and inaccuracies in this book: Pierre Audrit, Philippe Capelle, Vincent Demarneffe, Tim Harrup, Thierry Keutgen, Françoise Labaye, Gabrielle Leyden, Colette Michel, Colin Michel, Denis Michel, Renaud Michel, Éric Rozenberg, and Xavier Spirlet. If any errors remain, they are my fault, not theirs!

Made in the USA
San Bernardino, CA
22 December 2019